Don't Worry!
The Nigga Won't Read This

Own who you are. Own where you are.

Own where you are going.

Victor G. Maurice, Jr.

Don't Worry. The Nigga Won't Read This.

Copyright © 2014 Victor G. Maurice, Jr.

Revised 2017

All rights reserved.

ISBN: 1494941910

ISBN-13: 978-1494941918

Don't Worry. The Nigga Won't Read This.

DEDICATION

This book is dedicated to the most excellent manifestation of the Maker purposing my life. MY CHILDREN.

It is your existence that proves my purpose on this earth. You are my fruit. You are my multiplication. Now it is time for me to share with you how to subdue this land that OUR Maker has so graciously blessed us with.

It is His great pleasure, my children, that you enjoy the fullness of his creation. He made it for you, and as much as I would want to see you enjoy a gift that I have given you, it is even much more your Maker's enjoyment, to watch you enjoy the fullness of His love. This love is the most perfect gift that you will ever receive. Your Maker so loved you, that He graciously placed choice before you, and at the same time, prepared a provision of repentance for you when you make the choice that is contrary to what He made you to be.

Along the way you will encounter situations that will perplex you. You will be burdened with trouble along the way, even when you feel as if you had it all figured out. Don't be dismayed when you find yourself in the middle of a mess that seems too big, even for you to handle. It is during these times that the greatness in you must be revealed, so fret not.

Now, you have been made aware of the source, so there will be no doubt allowed amongst you. The same Maker that took me on the backside of the mountain to show himself to me, will be there with you as you traverse the dark times of life. These valley experiences will be necessary to show forth the power of his light in your life.

He will soon give you the choice for him to become YOUR God.

This choice will not ride in triumphantly to reveal himself to you. This choice will come when the pressures of living in this world, comes up against your purpose. It is in this choice where you will be made known of your true citizenship. At the revelation of this choice, you will be afforded the opportunity to develop the understanding necessary to operate in this world and not of this world. It will be your purpose's opposition to your current position in this world, that will present the opportunity for your Maker to truly reveal his most perfect and divine will in YOU, his most special creation.

You see, His strength will only be made perfect in your life during your most weakest moments. The closer you get to the light that reveals your purpose, the further in the distance the darkness of doubt and fear you were dreading, fades away.

Be the man or woman your Maker has called you to be. Do all things to live at peace with all men and in all things you do, you do it in love.

I know you will read this book, and I know I only have to tell you that a word is a word until you fill it up with the intent of your heart. Be powerful in your intent, with actions. Don't you dare concern yourself with impressing anyone. You owe him nothing but to love him.

You are a king of the King my son. You are a Queen of the King my daughter. There is no power on this earth that can ever remove you from the inheritance of your royalty. All that is for you will be given unto you. It is your purpose to focus on giving. So in every decision you make, consider if the end result is unto giving or receiving.
It is important to me that you remember the God of your father and mother. It is important to me that you remember the God of your grandmother. Yet, it is my sole purpose in life to see to it that you walk with YOUR God. He will always be doing new things.

I pray for you every night. I think of you every day. I love you guys with all of my heart. I love you because the Maker loved me so much so, that He gave you to my stewardship.

I am not your provider. I am your introduction to your provider. I am not your savior. I am your introduction to the One who saved me. I am not your reason. I am your introduction to the One who reasoned it all.

Remember always the answer is within. READ!!! HEAR!! READ SOME MORE!!!, and then search for the truth within yourself. It is the spirit that is within you that teaches, so try the spirit with the spirit and see if it be true, and remember when I see each of you, you better have memorized that scripture. :)

"And we know that all things work together for good to them that love God, to them who are the called according to his purpose."
Romans 8:28

TABLE OF CONTENTS

Foreward……………………………………………..

Preface …………………………………………………..

Introduction …………………………………………….

Ch 1. Dear My Nigga ……………………………….

Ch 2. What's in the word Nigga? ………………….

Ch 3. War of the Worlds …………………………….

Ch 4. Battlefield of the Mind ………………………

Ch 5. The New Slave Master……………………….

Ch 6. Own Who you are ……………………………..

CH 7. Own Where You Are………………………..

Ch 8. Own Where You Are Going………………

CH 9. Now Faith Is ………………………………..

FOREWORD

I often pondered the necessity to title this book "Don't Worry. The Nigga Won't Read This". Even after my first publishing of this book, I wrestled with the thought that maybe the title was a 'turn off' and it would cause the book to be overlooked as a work of 'ignorance' by those that "mattered"... and then I prayed.

I entered that prayer session with the thought that maybe this work was 'ruined' out the gate and the anticipation that I would get the "OK" to rewrite and rename this work in hopes that it would be more palatable to the 'wise' that I, in myself, was seeking approval from. I was sure my Maker would affirm my desire to be an inspirational impact on the world and prove the doubt that I was feeling in myself, by sending a still small voice to say "O.K. Change it".

I knew that the title always seemed like 'sumn Vic would do'. I did, often times, feel apprehensive when I introduced or discussed this work with those 'Vic' was seeking to win approval from. So I prayed.

I prayed for over 4 yrs waiting on the day I knew that "this was the day" I would begin to rewrite and rename this book. Life came and went and it's daily ups and downs made demands that often times presented the thought that I was just a "conform" away from "them" accepting me, and my assimilation into who "they" say I am would make all of my troubles disappear. But I prayed.

I prayed for the easy way in and I got the mandate to be the one to call out. I prayed for "them" to accept me and it became clear that "they" have a plan that implicitly excluded me. I prayed that "we" would both benefit from this book and realized that "they" have a predetermined use for "us". I prayed for the "other way" to start this conversation and my answer came in the same manner and with the same authority that compelled me to write this book.

Simply… Don't Worry. The Nigga Won't Read This.

So here I am at the beginning of a "That's sumn Vic would do" run for a seat as a U.S. Senator representing the great state of Mississippi, and I am more certain than ever that this work was given its title, in the maturation of my message. to be there standing tall at the presentation of my message. That simple message of OWNING who you are, OWNING where you are, and OWNING where you are going is something "They" nigga would never do, but it's the ONLY thing "My" nigga has in his mind to do.

I prayed for the generations before me to understand that "Fighting for your rights" makes no sense if you can't clearly define your enemy whose intent is to withhold those rights and I was ordered to instruct the generations after me to KNOW their rights... because NOT KNOWING is their enemy. I was taught to pray for my storehouse to be full, and I have matured to know that a full storehouse requires workers in the field.

The harvest of a healed America in the 21st century is plentiful NOW but the laborers are few.

Identifiers like "Liberal" and "Conservative", "Democrat" and "Republican", or "American" and "African American" has caused an ever growing need to divide, and as a WHOLE PEOPLE, we have suffered the stain of who "They" say we are for far too long. This focus on unfruitfulness has made the effectiveness of the seed secondary to the ignorance of "We" good and "They" bad, as we faint for the temporal stimulation of our taste buds.

Good fruit and Bad fruit have one thing in common… they both possess in it's seed a potential tree to produce more enjoyment than the best tasting fruit can ever offer.

I have ended my prayer session on this matter. I have received my answer and I am confident in this one thing…

The God who has begun a good work in America SHALL complete it.

So keep your eyes on where the manure lies, for in it you will find the ideal place for a fruitful tree.
Here's to reaping the harvest prepared for "US" that "THEY" can not deny. #BeGreat

PREFACE

It is not wise to believe that you live, breathe, and conduct your being under your own power. It is this realization that pushed me to write this book.

I began this journey at the most terrible time of my life. I had lost it all, it seemed, and the truth of the statement "Once you hit bottom, there is no way to go but up" was my only motivation.

It was the fact that I had seen, without a doubt, hell on earth and the only thing I had to grab onto was the God of my mother. Her God had been here before, and her God had, in 3 days, conquered this barren place and went UP! I decided that getting to my mother's God would be my motivation.

That sounded good... in theory. But ohh, my friend, It was the practice of this theory, that I concluded in my own mind and followed in my own understanding, that I would struggle with.

You see, all lessons are learned through observation and practice. You must first observe the action with your senses and then translate that into effective action, only through the trial and error of practice.

My mother's God's instructions went something like this:

"For whosoever shall call upon the name of the Lord shall be saved. How then shall they call on him in whom they have not believed? And how shall they believe in him of whom they have not heard? And how shall they hear without a preacher? And how shall they preach, except they be sent? As it is written, How beautiful are the feet of them that preach the gospel of peace, and bring glad tidings of good things!" Romans 10:13-15

>Ok. Call on Him. Got that. Check.

When I called up on him I was saved from this hell. Yes?
Of Course I was. The question is, though, after I called did I walk in that belief?

Mother's God went on to explain to me before the call ended, that during those times that I called out in travail while I suffered, absent from His light, stuck in this hell on earth, that I wasn't calling out at all to Him, because I didn't know Him. I only knew of Him. I didn't know Him. I wasn't intimate with Him. I wasn't familiar with Him, and on the word of His sovereignty, He is not compelled to respond to me.

He saved me because I called out to my mother's God. His prosperity and progression in my life after He "saved" me, was solely predicated upon how well I knew Him.
Now it was good to be saved, but my ability to make that next call, and the call after that, had a prerequisite.

I must get to know Him.

How then can I get to know this God to believe in Him so I can call on Him, unless I heard (perceived, inquired, and acclimated) the instructions from a preacher on how to get to know Him? And how will I be properly instructed unless the One I am looking to get to know sends the preacher.

OHHH how beautiful are the feet of the one who brings me these instructions. But who is this person and what's taking them so long?
I looked to make a 3 way call, first, through the preachers I knew of. I must admit that this quest opened me up to hope, but it was short lived when the fullness of what I was looking for couldn't be instructed by the preacher I went to.

I looked to make a call through my family line, but all the lines were busy as they were all tied up with people trying to make calls of their own.

I looked around, for a good many of years I realize now, for somebody, anybody, that would let me use their line to make a call.

Even if someone was willing to let me use their phone, the number I was trying to dial required a different type connection, and my attempts to reach my Mother's God only led to my actions running their phone bill up to the point that it fractured my relationship with them. I left every house I sought refuge in, worse off, more than it was when I came to the house in my distress.

I HAD ENOUGH.

I had the chance to use my mother's phone one more time, moments before she coded in the hospital, and passed away, on Sept 18, 2013. It was on that call to her God, that I got the last instructions my Mother's God would ever give me.

My Mother's God advised me that I should be still, and wait on a very quiet spirit that will visit me, in due season, to instruct me. He also told me, on that call, that after I hung up this specific line, I would no longer have access to my mother's God.

He ended the call with these words explaining to me what was to happen after he sent his messenger, his tabernacle, his spirit, to dwell with me:

"If ye walk in my statutes, and keep my commandments, and do them; then I will give you rain in due season, and the land shall yield her increase, and the trees of the field shall yield their fruit. And your threshing shall reach unto the vintage, and the vintage shall reach unto the sowing time: and ye shall eat your bread to the full, and dwell in your land safely. And I will give peace in the land, and ye shall lie down, and none shall make you afraid: and I will rid evil beasts out of the land, neither shall the sword go through your land. And ye shall chase your enemies, and they shall fall before you by the sword. And five of you shall chase an hundred, and an hundred of you shall put ten thousand to flight: and your enemies shall fall before you by the sword. For I will have respect unto you, and make you fruitful, and multiply you, and establish my covenant with you. And ye shall eat old store, and bring forth the old because of the new. And I set my tabernacle among you: and my soul shall not abhor you. And I will walk among you, and will be **YOUR** God, and ye shall be **MY** people. I am the LORD your God, which brought you forth out of the land of Egypt, that ye should not be their bondmen; and I have broken the bands of your yoke, and made you go upright.". Leviticus 3:13

He became MY God.

What a burden lifter! My hell disappeared immediately as the light of my messenger, sent to comfort and instruct, drew nigh unto me.

No longer did I have a need, or desire, to seek to use someone else's phone. I had the instructor with me.
You see, I was looking for the gospel through my observation of those who professed THEIR gospel as the way for me. I didn't understand, in wisdom that it was the way for them.

I am not negating the gospel that anyone professes, but it became very evident when I would try to model my life after my observation of others operating in their gospel, is when I experienced the most pain; as the power of their gospel was limited in my life.

It was temporal. It was subject to my ability to connect to the power in accordance with their gospel. It became a matter of life or death that I be sent a preacher. It was divine order that this messenger be perfectly equipped to instruct VICTOR.

Hear me closely, please. There is no made creature that is equipped to teach you the fullness of your purpose. They can only point you in a direction, and it is on you to seek out that way to see if it is the right direction… for you.

They can only allow you to use their phone to make a call. It's on you to get to the place where he has designated a line for you. It is there where you will meet your instructor. It is in this place where you will know Him.

You will not fulfill your purpose seeking the instructions of another person's maker. You will never run the race at your max ability relying on someone else's coach. You will not become acquainted with the awesomeness of the heaven that has been prepared for you, on this earth, if you spend your time scouting, coveting, and basing your existence on the charity of your neighbor's kingdom.

You must discover your OWN God. You must consult your OWN coach. You must scout and develop, in earnest, your OWN kingdom.

This is why I wrote this book. I wrote this book to be a messenger from your Maker to let you know that He has heard your call. I wrote this book to encourage you as you search inside yourself, for the true meaning of YOUR life. I wrote this book because as I search out my purpose, my instructions compel me to announce that your voice has been heard and that He has not forgotten that which He has ordained.

The greatness you seek, is in you. This greatness is even greater than anything that would ever oppose you from searching out how great the greatness inside of you is.

Take heart as you read through this book, knowing that when you called, He saved you and sent you a preacher. This preacher is unique to you and can only be found in you. Learn from this preacher how to live according to the gospel, or good news, that the preacher sent to you, just for you, professes.

Stay with the preacher. Take the preacher with you. So when you need to get to the Maker, the preacher will show you just what to do, so all of the things that happen in your life, will be caused to work together for your good. All because you were called out (heard the call, responded in acceptance, and faithfully moved towards), according to your Maker's purpose and perfect will for your existence.

You knew of Him. Now you will know Him… for YOURSELF.

Don't Worry. The Nigga Won't Read This.

Hear me, as I call from the desert experience of my life, that was necessary to cement my Maker's will in my life. Hear me announce that what you seek to know was placed inside of you in the beginning, so turn around and go back to the beginning.

Seek out your beginning, within yourself, and it will be the revelation of your beginning that will carry you to your expected end. Where you began is the place where you will also realize your access. Know this, because you don't know in your own understanding, where you began; it is important that a preacher be sent to reveal this secret place to you.

The connection to the source has a beginning, and it will be revealed by the preacher that was sent to you. You don't have to yell out in hopeless despair anymore. When the preacher connects your understanding to your Maker, then you will have established the validity of your connection to your purposed source, and you will be FREE to draw upon that source as the source allows.

Let me bring this point home real clearly for you.

You can call out to Jay-Z if you just so happen to see him, but you can not call upon Jay-Z to come to your side, unless you know him. And you can not come to know Jay-Z, unless a source that is familiar with Jay-Z instructs you on how to get to him. If Jay-Z does not ordain the messenger to establish the proper communications channel, then the message you believed in, is not valid.

It's only until the messenger connects you to Jay-Z, that you believe that you have access to get to know Jay-Z, and in knowing him, you can experience the gift of Jay-Z's love.

Your connection validated your messenger.

Now, until you become intimate with Jay-Z, it is wise to consult your messenger as to how to approach Jay-Z, and unless Jay-Z decides to call you himself, it will be that messenger who brings you the news concerning your relationship with Jay-Z.

I wrote this book to bear witness to the Maker, and how He has walked down through time to hear your cry and cause you to be drawn unto Him.

WHY? Because now is the appointed time for you to GROW and GO. The time for travailing and wailing in agony is over.

I am lead to inform you that your EMANCIPATION PROCLAMATION has been written on your heart. READ IT!

Your preacher is there to help you understand all the legal mumbo jumbo. YOU ARE FREE. So feel free to cast your cares on your source. Feel free to be filled, because as He fills you, He will overflow you and cause your cup to run over so others can taste and see that He is good.

    This book is my overflow in this area. I pray you taste and see that it is good.

    Real Talk. RNS.

Don't Worry. The Nigga Won't Read This.

INTRODUCTION

Is there hope for the African American Male?

It is said that a black man is born with two strikes already counted against him; the strike of being black, and the strike of being a black man.

Throughout my youth, I played baseball. I revelled in learning the game in what would be perceived as an unorthodox way. My experience gathered during my growth in this game, gave me great awareness in my ability to overcome the perceived NO-NO's and restrictions the game presented to my unique position as a player.

From my beginnings as an All Star left handed catcher in the local dixie youth league to excelling competitively, as the 1st baseman on my high school team (my coach didn't want a left handed catcher… DREAM KILLER!! lol), there were many times I found myself at the plate having to deal with the dilemma of a stressful at-bat, being 2 strikes down.

Now, I must admit, having those two strikes against me did cause a level of uneasiness, uncertainty, and doubt concerning my ability to have a successful at bat, but more times than not, when I stepped out of the batter's box to gather my composure, I would step back up to the plate with a renewed confidence in my ability to put the ball in play to give myself, and more importantly my team, the opportunity to be in a better position to advance the runners that were on base to the next base, and ultimately on to score a run.

This book is written to give the reader the assurance that they too can take a step out of the batter's box of life, gather themselves, and have a successful at bat. It is my most sincere desire, that the reader understands with a great degree of certainty, that the confidence he will need to put the ball in play, has been programmed into his DNA, and that his self-confidence has been taking batting practice in the batting cage of life preparing, often out of the sheer need for survival, to have a successful at-bat, in the face of 2 strikes.

Every time life threw him a curveball, his confidence would learn to sit on the pitch and be patient, as he made the adjustment to impact the ball. After having seen many change-ups thrown at him, he would learn; if he committed to being a student of the game; to keep his hands back and judge the speed of the ball. He would be able to determine, through his trained sense of observation, that the pitch was coming as fast, or as slow, as the last pitch.

He will know to be anxious for nothing concerning how fast or slow the pitch is coming. It will be his experience, that was refined by the instruction of his coach, that will make him aware, as his game time instincts begin to implement the drills he worked on in practice. He will know, or become intimate with the understanding that he has but to make the adjustment, in the same manner that he did while practicing for this moment. He will be able to confidently take his at bat, and produce the results he desired when he stepped to the plate, not simply because he was great, but because he submitted, in earnest, to being a student that was attentive and committed in application, to the coach's instructions on the practice field to operating effectively in his GREATNESS.
.
Not everyone who plays the game of baseball will achieve the levels of the greats like Hank Aaron or Babe Ruth. It is true though, that everyone who commits to study the game of baseball, can become competent in his understanding of how to play the game. A focused student can be effective, on some level competitively, at the game, according to his level of commitment to understand the game in theory and application.

When you decide to commit to understanding the game of life, you will find that there is a designated domain assigned to an opposing force that the rules of the game require you to come up against during every minute the ball of life is in play. This opposition is vital to the integrity of the game and is very important to test your abilities as an individual player in some aspects, but more so to prove the ability of the team to work as a unit.

This book is written to encourage your individual play and to help you hone your skills as a player so you can be an effective member of the team. Your ability to play your position, with a level of mastery, is important to your team being victorious.

The opposing team to life has been successful at dominating other teams that have players on it with a skill set similar to, and often greater than yours, for years. This rival has learned the habits of these other players with little to no effort required, and exploited these habits on the field of life, to render them ineffective as a unit, and incapable of even putting runners on base, not to mention scoring a run.

Now is the time for you, and those on your team, to make the adjustments necessary. It is time to present a team that has corrected the mistakes, through focused study and determined application in practice, that were passed down to you by default, mainly in ignorance, from the players that played before you. It is time to put a new game plan together that takes the opposition by surprise.

The other team is not expecting you to make the adjustment on the change up. The opposing pitcher is confident in his curveball and will throw it as often as he can, believing that you can't hit it.

Now is the time to take your next practice sessions seriously, and condition your mind and body to be effective in offense, and relentless in defense. The big game is drawing near.
If you take the time to build yourself up in the understanding and application of the game, you will be successful.

YOU PLAY HOW YOU PRACTICE!

Every time you take your place in the batter's box and accept the fact that you are walking to the plate with 2 strikes, you will be confident in the fact that in this game, all it takes is one swing of the bat to put the ball in play.

Sit on the curve ball. Make the adjustment to the change up. You are the one with the bat. Don't chase the balls thrown to confuse you and to make you swing outside of your strike zone. The rules are the rules for the pitcher and batter alike. When you step up to the plate, understand that no pitcher has it in his mind to walk you unless he is scared that you will get a hit.

If life decides to pitch to you, which it will every time you step to the plate, take confidence in knowing that your preparation in practice, has made you more than capable to put the ball in play. Of course, only if the pitch thrown, is in your strike zone. BATTER UP!

Ye are of God, little children, and have overcome them: because greater is he that is in you, than he that is in the world. 1 John 4:4

DEAR MY NIGGA

As I lay here in this hospital bed, looking out the window at a construction crew laboring in the rising heat of the sun spread concrete for a new sidewalk that will be the landscape's focal point on the grounds of the VA Medical center in Biloxi, MS; my eyes focus on the group of African American men in the crew that are working, in tandem, like a choreographed dance, to pull the concrete dumped from the truck along the form of the sidewalk.

I am watching attentively at these men, partly because it is the only outside interference that I have, apart from laying in the hospital bed hoping for a decent show to come on the television hanging from the ceiling. I look to constructively occupy my thoughts and provide an escape from the melancholy mood that looms over a hospital room when you have no visitors and I long to break the monotony of listening to the beeps of the machine that are monitoring my vitals.

Not to mention that I am hard pressed to find the benefits associated with sharing a room with an old man who moans constantly because he can't pass gas, as he wallows in his accepted state of pain for at least another hour or so before any staff will make it back on their rounds, barring he (or I for that matter) codes before then.

I am engaged in my study of these men with intrigue, mostly because I happen to be fond of concrete work, seeing as how it is a profession that I have been blessed to have gathered some limited experience in in the past year or so leading up to this moment of my intense observation, as these men work in the hot sun, appearing to not allow the heat of the day to keep them from completing their mission.

I wonder, as I watch this group of men, and as I observe their body language from afar, if their conversation, while they 'pour out', is similar to the ones I would have with the fellas I work with, when we gather around to 'pour out' when the concrete truck arrives. I wonder, in myself, if their conversation is about what they are going to do in the next few hours after the job has been finished?

After all, when the cement truck comes, the money isn't too far behind.

I wonder if their entire payout for this job is already spoken for by past due bills and looming debt, as mine were? I wonder if they even knew the next time they would have a float or a trial tool in their hand?

I hope, with very little confidence, that they were talking about their next job or their next investment move, but the odds are, sadly, that their conversation was probably much the same as the ones I've had while floating concrete with other guys in this area many times before.

No talk of the current political affairs of the country, state or even local municipality. I am almost certain there was little mention, if any, even of the grand scope of the project that they were but laborers on. No thoughts or consideration during their conversation, I am sure, as to how they can be the contractor and not just show up on the site as contracted labor.

Unfortunately, that's not the conversation... stereo-typically.

Often times these guys show up to the site in a vehicle that has a near empty tank of gas. Many of them just left an uncomfortable financial situation at home and bringing some calm to that storm raging on the home front consuming their relationships on all sides, is most likely, the dominant thought in that laborers mind.

The "Baby Momma" has been calling for the past few days, complaining about how he never does anything for his child. The Landlord has put the pay or quit notice on the door because he is late on his rent for the 3rd month in a row. His insurance has lapsed on his vehicle and he fears being pulled over by the police because he has old fines.

This one payout will probably buy him some time with the landlord. A couple of dollars will ease the bear in his baby momma. He may make a payment on his fines. He most likely will forgo the thought of insurance and pray his driving skills hold up and keep him from being stopped by the police.

The odds are, only one of these scenarios will get any attention and the cycle will appear to never end because as soon as you correct one issue, it's either a recurring event or it will immediately be replaced by another, often times more stressful problem.

I wonder, as I watch this brother, pull a bull float over the concrete to level it out with precision, what is going through his mind as he makes every effort to focus on the task at hand. I stand, looking out this hospital window, almost longing to be 'in the mud' with these strangers, as I try to decipher the thoughts of the man edging the curb.

Where does this skilled laborer look to get the answers to the problems he faced? Does he have a mentor in his life that instructs him, on a personal level? Is his information source for dealing with the trials of life, as rich as the one which instructed him in the trade he executed with precision?

I wonder does he even take time, in the face of all he does simply in the name of survival, to read a book, any book, that could give him insight into the proper construction and management of the things in his life that seem to weigh him down even after he has committed to doing, in earnest, all he knows how to do?

Hell, I wonder, in pity, if the brother even knows how to read?

I wonder if he knew the words that he couldn't find to use to express to his fellow laborer about how he aspired to be greater than just a concrete finisher, could be found hidden, in plain sight, in a book somewhere? I wonder if given the proper introduction, if he would read this book?

I wonder if I used big words, if this book would impress upon the 'learned' ones and my writings become just another literary piece that failed to reach its true intended target... that laborer?

I wonder how I can tell my fellow laborer that he was a CHAMPION, that he was a WINNER, that he was THE BEST OF THE BEST?

I wonder if my brother felt he should read this book? I wonder if my homie could read this book? I wonder if my NIGGA would read this book?

So I write this book for my NIGGA!

It is my earnest desire that you, My Nigga, come to the full understanding of how awesome you really are. I pray, without ceasing throughout this process, that each and every one of you find that one nugget of hope that solidifies your faith that 'There is gold in them, there hills!'

This book will not make you rich. This book will not answer every problem that you encounter. This book is but a flashing light as you go along your journey to be an established mile marker that assures you that where you are, is closer to your end goal, more than where you were before you decided to read this book.

I can not stress enough the importance of you honing your ability to understand life through reading. What you see has the most profound effect on what you believe. When you hear the news it can move you, but when you see the event happening, it will affect you.

Words are but pictures for the inner man to process the current state he is in. It is his understanding of the word that will develop inside of him, the assurance that he is in the right place. If he gets little word concerning his condition or place in life, he will expect little out of his condition or place in life. His fear will overwhelm him, paralyzing him more and more, preventing him from moving in faithful expectation.

Would you agree that the more words you come to know and understand, the more confident you become in the use of the english language?

Is it safe to say that the more words you understand concerning your job will lend to you being more confident in your actions to effectively complete your tasks at work?

Can a mechanic truly be efficient if he has no understanding of the word 'catalytic converter'? If the mental picture in his mind is limited only to the awareness of the object the word 'catalytic converter' represents, is it possible for the mechanic to truly be a mechanic without the understanding of the fullness of the word? Can the mechanic who is equipped only with the understanding of what a catalytic converter looks like, in faith, take on the task of repairing the part, if he has no understanding of what the thing described is converting? If he didn't understand all of the aspects of this part, and how it worked in concert, purposefully, to affect the overall effectiveness of the vehicle, the mechanic could only hope that his actions will produce the desired result.

When the mechanic makes the choice to operate in this ignorance of hope, all it will take is one problem to transfer him from the emotional state of hope, to the bondage of fear. The mechanic will be forced to continue his task under that emotion or make a conscious decision to quit the task all together in defeat, or to take the steps necessary to gain the understanding through study of some sort, on how to properly complete the task.

This book was written with the hope of you making the latter decision and submit yourself to be taught of the greatness that lies inside of you.

Being a shade tree mechanic did not affect the business building of that mechanic until he accepted the socially projected image and practice of a shade tree mechanic as his own. At that point of acceptance, everything that would be attracted to his business would be the business that is suitable for a shade tree mechanic. Try as he may, until he projected in thought and actions that he was not just a shade tree mechanic and that he just happened to be a mechanic that conducted his work under the shade of the tree, he would always be subject to the rewards of a shade tree mechanic, because that is what he resolved, in himself, to be.

When the mechanic decides to take the steps to change his mind concerning the label that was ascribed to him, you can expect that the type of business he attracted would change. He would learn to use the struggle as leverage in the execution of his purpose, and cause even his given label to work together for his good. This conscious decision could very well be the opposing force necessary to change even the meaning of the label that was ascribed to him.

What a sight to see, when the shade tree mechanic becomes owner of a chain of mechanic shops, that he decided, in honor of his transformed meaning of the word that was negatively ascribed to him, to name his business, aptly, Shade Tree and Sons, LLC.

You see, being a nigga wasn't a problem, until I said ok I'll be that. I accepted their label and acted accordingly, as I suffered through the pain of being the type of nigga, the label impressed upon me. Being called a thug wasn't a problem, until I said ok i'll be that. I accepted the label and did, in primal fear of loss, the things that the socially accepted meaning of thug afforded.

Now that I'm finding out I'm more than just a Nigga Thug... WHAT'S THE PROBLEM?"

Define your understanding of the word in your life. In your understanding will lie the tools that lend to you achieving your defined result. If your results, in the use of the word that you have been given, are contrary to your desired results, then your understanding must be refined. It is your understanding that must be refined, like gold in the fire, to be considered and used at its highest worth.

It is not the social understanding of anything that will produce results in your life, it is YOUR understanding of the thing, itself, that will produce the results in your life. Your understanding must be tested. it must be tried, even in the fire of life's opposition, to prove its fullness through your pursuit of purpose.

Just as the conviction of the forefathers of America had to be tried by the fire of slavery to prove that all men truly were created equal, so must your conviction be tried to prove that you are who you were made to be.

When your expectations of your life, don't seem to align up with your position in life, it is mandatory that you submit to the will of change. You must allow the areas of your life that are operating in ignorance, to be filled with the know-how to experience the full weight, or glory, of the love that fulfills the purpose your internal compass points to.

Know yourself, My Nigga.

Make every effort to keep your mind geared towards knowing, because in seeking to know, you will be equipped with the power to be known. You can not fill yourself. It is of the utmost, that you seek knowledge. It is mandatory that you learn to become effective with the awesome power that dwells in you. Awake the giant in wisdom. Promote the giant in you with your zeal to know and not be known. Purpose the giant in you with the understanding that, even as great a giant you are, even you were created, as a giant, for an even greater purpose. Don't just roam, a giant in the land, being destructive because you failed to truly understand your greatness.

In all of your quest to get knowledge to affirm your mastery, in theory, of the matter, set your end compass on understanding. Get understanding.

In your pursuit of knowledge to know all of the things that are possible by man, there's an even higher purpose to understand, that answers the why of what who did, when or where, and how they did it.

I know you wanna know WHY you are a nigga huh?

My answer to you can only be a pointer to the solution I found that worked for me. I can not make you believe that it will work for you. I believe it will work for you… so I point.

This is my testimony to you. I believe that greater is He that is within me, than he that is in the force that opposes me. I found out He was in me when I grew tired of looking all over the world outside of me.

I suggest you look inside of you. I write this book because I believe that the power that dwells dormant in you, is greater than the opposition you encounter outside of you. From here on out it's on you. What I have I will give. In the name of the one who paid the price for everything I destroyed along my path to know and understand, rise up, and walk into your season.

"Uh, no slacking, no beggin, no askin, no fastin. No disrespect to Islam or Iman or Pastor. No answers to questions the media's asking. While we fight each other in public in front of these arrogant fascists. They love it; putting the old niggaz versus the youngest. Most of our elders failed us, how could they judge us? Niggaz! There's verbal books published by niggaz, produced by niggaz. Genuine niggaz, so I salute my niggaz..." Nas

CHAPTER 2

What's in the word NIGGA?

Don't Worry. The Nigga Won't Read This.

WHAT'S IN THE WORD NIGGA?

There is so much power in a word, that it is virtually impossible to limit it to one simple instance. To make an attempt to identify an object's content by its packaging is speculation, at best.

Not every blue box that has Tiffany & Co on it, holds in it, jewelry made by Tiffany & Co.

They say it's not wise to judge a book by its cover, so I offer that same train of thought as we open the word NIGGA and see what's inside.

Words are, in their simplest form, cargo vessels that transport intent from its source of origin to its predefined destination.

In another way, words ain't worth much, if what you mean by it, can't be figured out by the person you are saying it to.

God is still God to those who call Him God, even if another person use the word container god to identify another god that is not their all ruling God. Love is still love whether you're talking about making love, showing love, or being in love.

So If I can understand the wordsmith's intent, by analyzing the container's content, then nigga can be nigga to me, in context, different than it is to someone else, whose intended use is manifested in a different context.

'My nigga...', whose presence is announced with endearment, is an entirely different nigga than an ill-willed speaker's understanding and use of nigga, whose intent was to show the content in a negative state, often used to force the subject into a mental place of submission "That nigga..."

It amazes me, the effort and energy, that society wastes trying to rid itself of the word NIGGA. The funny thing is until it became an accepted label by young men as a badge of POWER, the use of the word NIGGA was far from a hot social issue as it was cast to the side, out of the eyesight of social concern, because those who were appointed that label or accepted that label were of little importance in the grand scheme of the accepted social order.

Now that I, in my heart, have groomed an affinity for the word, and its meaning to me is not negating but uplifting; the same society has mustered the efforts of even my elders to strip from me, the ability to feel empowered by my OWN definition of the word.

The social order, fueled by the spirit of control, is doing everything it can to defy the redefining of this word. It is unacceptable to them, that we have adopted this term and redefined it, because still in their mind, the word is filled with hate and ill will. Little do they know, perceive or understand, that I have chosen to empty out this word container that was given to me, and fill it with love and adoration to give me hope that even the thing that was designed for my bad, can be used for my good.

Consider the word CHRISTIAN. If I was to tell you that there is no where in the HOLY BIBLE that refers to the use of this word in a positive manner, would you believe me?

I would venture to say that you probably would be skeptical at the least and outright in protest if I was to make that assessment. If this is the case and you are one of the 'non-believers' of this statement, you have my permission to close this book right now, fall back on your skepticism, and start your protesting because that is exactly what I am saying.

The word Christian is used 3 times in the bible, and with a little emphasis added to help drive my point home, I will discuss these 3 verses now.

<u>Acts 11:26</u>

"And when he(*Barnabus*) had found him (*Paul*), he brought him unto

Antioch. And it came to pass, that a whole year they assembled themselves with the church, and taught much people. *(In a place that was socially despondent to the new outlook on life the Apostles spoke of)* And the disciples were called Christians first in Antioch.

They were called Christians. They did not call themselves Christians. 'Those CHRISTIANS.'

Acts 26:28

"Then Agrippa said unto Paul, Almost thou persuadest me to be a Christian."

This occurrence is after Paul had been summoned by the king to give account to the accusations the jewish society brought against him for supposedly violating their custom laws. Paul spoke from his heart concerning the power that transformed him on the Damascus Road where his zealous pursuit of significance amongst the believers of his inherited religion had met, face to face, with the real reason he was gifted with such a zeal.

This revelation was not given to him to affect his religion that man accounted unto him according to his birthright. It was given to accomplish his PURPOSE. That purpose being to bear witness around the region of the power source that caused the divine interference on that road. To testify of that power that changed even his name, in an instance, from Saul to Paul.

Agrippa, the king whose word is final in his domain, had, but if for a moment, considered that he would be better off had he been a CHRISTIAN.

1 Peter 4:16

"Yet if any man suffer as a Christian, let him not be ashamed; but let him glorify God on this behalf."

The Apostle Peter offered this statement in the context of enduring trials and hardships as you live your life striving to live on purpose. He exhorts the reader to not consider it strange that they find themselves in a fiery trial along their journey. He encourages the reader to rejoice because you have been graced to endure this appointed struggle to shew forth that same power that met Paul on the Damascus Road, in fullness, in their life as well.

He goes on to impress upon the reader that none of them should suffer as (like, even as, having adopted the label of) a murderer, or a thief, or an evildoer, or someone who makes himself busy concerning himself with the manners of others (during this age we call these people NOSEY or HATERS to be more precise), yet if they should be called upon to suffer as a CHRISTIAN (the derogatory name used by the people of that day to label those who have publicly declared allegiance to that false prophet Jesus) should not be ashamed (Don't trip my NIGGA) but glory in that power that allowed this Damascus Road experience in their life, to reveal and refine the PURPOSE that was placed in you before you were ever formed in your mother's womb.

So in this spirit I write this book... to share truth, as I have experienced it, with MY NIGGAS.

I speak, as humble as I know how, to my brother of the struggle, to my nigga who looks around and can see no hand up, in the midst of many hand outs that have strings attached to them. I mourn for my niggas, who want more but don't know what more looks like. I write to share with my nigga, whose initial hopes of progress were limited to a few stories of someone who 'made it out', and where unfortunately suffocated by the appeal of ill gotten fortunes of dope dealing and mind manipulation.

I am writing this with my nigga in mind, who fell victim to the lies of the streets, the lies that were yelled, with much conviction, " You ain't nothing... but a no good NIGGA."

I write to encourage my nigga, who in the midst of all the madness, looks to find comfort, often times in vain, in his niggas who he thought had vowed, to stick closer to him than a brother.

I write to promote the efforts of my nigga, who shared his visions of greatness with his brothers of the struggle in confidence, only to have his vision shot down, deprived of any kind of brotherly support, and die a horrific death on the threshing floor of peer opinion, before the vision even took root in his spirit.

I write to reignite the fire of my nigga, who was the great-great-great-great grandson of a slave, and the great grandson of a 'FREED MAN' who had no idea what freedom truly was.

I write this book, with my nigga in mind, who has no clue of who his grandfather even was and often times can't tell you the middle name of his father.

I write, in faith, to my nigga, to let him know that there is a crown of royalty assigned to him before the foundations of the earth were laid.

I write to let him know that whom the Son set free is truly free indeed.

For what seems like all of my life, I have combated with the affinity I felt in the word NIGGA when I used it and the hate that was associated with its contents by others who didn't have the same understanding of the word as I did.

It was a bipolar type experience as I loved and hated the word at the same time.

It was all first dependent upon who said it. Then as the cultural influence on my life evolved, it became more about what the intent of the person who said it was.

I had white friends who I called My Nigga. They called me My Nigga. This presented an even deeper problem because I could no longer limit my understanding of the power of this word and my accepted belief of its use, to be based solely upon the color of the speaker's skin.

But that's how I was taught and this teaching is what was supposed to be my doctrine on the matter, No?

The word was good to me, and pain to me at the same time.

I felt like Tity 2-Chainz, I was loving it and hating it at the same damn time. What do I do? I can't love it and hate it at the same time can I? If it is what it is; unless I live double-minded; I had to either love it or hate it.

It was in this trial, that I discovered the truth for Victor concerning the matter.

I discovered that it was not what I heard that my doctrine was based off of. I found that it was what I saw, what I experienced when the sound wrote its intent on my heart. It was the fullness of the picture that formed on my heart, that gave liberty to my mind to ascribe a certain emotion to it.

The power of the word had to first be defined clearly in my heart, my belief zone. My operation protocol that assigned whatever emotion to the word, was not activated by the word, but by the belief my heart commanded, according to conditioning, to immerse my mental make up in.

It was at this crossroad that I faced the choice of but one of two ways. Either I could continue in this bipolar state and be unstable in all my ways, or I can recondition my protocol to respond in a way that is more favorable to what I believe the word to mean in me.

So I did just that.

I decided that every time I hear the word NIGGA that I would smile. Immediately, with that smile, any ill will associated with this word package, would be of no effect in my life. I decided that every time I heard this word that it was a gift in some fashion or another, to either encourage me in love, or instruct me in love.

This word would become a win-win in my life because if I detected encouragement I would be empowered because My Nigga cared enough to give it to me. Consequently, if I detected ill-will, I would consider it instruction in observing the truth that no weapon formed against me shall prosper.

Either way I received the gift in love, and understood that because I was allowed to hear it, I am even more responsible for making sure my response either builds on the love or I should replace the content of the package with my belief of love before I transferred the full image to my emotional control center.

So please, My Nigga, read on. There is so much in store for you as a king of the King. There is so much for you to accomplish as master of your domain. There are uncharted seas to be navigated as captain of your own ship. These words I pen for you, My Nigga.

So that you will know, in yourself, that it's not the word in itself that has the power, but It's the faith in the word, that has the power.

Greater is He that is in you, my nigga, than he that is in this world.

PURPOSEFUL POWER!!! That's what you have been looking for. Now you know where it is.

IT'S IN YOU!

"I'm not saying I'm gonna change the world, but I guarantee that I will spark the brain that will change the world" Tupac Shakur

CHAPTER 3
War of the Worlds

WAR OF THE WORLDS

Let's see... what's going on in the world today as I write? The year is 2013 and the country is making every effort to recover from the biggest economic recession since the great depression. Unemployment remains high. The price of gas is near $4.00 a gallon. The housing market is in shambles and the world social climate is held hostage by the threat of global terrorism.

Barack Obama is serving his second term as the first black President of the United States of America but the political climate is so overtly polarized, one would think the country was still living in the spirit of the civil rights era.

Schools are integrated but the overall assessment of the African American student shows the poorest scholastic levels since the formative years following the civil war.

The ideal of slavery is such a negative thought in the minds of the people, that they make every effort to act as if slavery didn't exist. It's safe, then, to assume that the prevailing sentiment on the matter is out of sight, out of mind.

As a nation politically, we do all we can to paint over the scars that fester still today, with compromising legislation like Affirmative Action and social programs like welfare, that in their most valiant attempt, can only place a band aid on the hemorrhaging wounds caused by the institution of slavery in the United States of America.

I am not calling these programs useless. I am calling these programs what they are; temporary fixes that are misunderstood and misused as a permanent crutch. I have been a beneficiary of welfare in some fashion all of my life.

Dependency on the government is no different than dependency on anything else. And to be honest, up unto my source from others ran out, I was just as comfortable chasing a welfare check, trying to manipulate the system for as long as the law would allow. I was determined, with a misdirected zeal, to apply for aid to anyone that would stop this bleeding, that would no doubt bring my existence to an end.

The problem I found, when I woke up in the pig pen of despair, was that I had formed my definition of independence on my selfish dependency for an outside force to do for me, only what I was responsible for doing for myself.

My emotions that managed my desire for control had been all crossed up. I fought to get another to do for me. I cried to get another to do for me. I begged to get another for me. I longed to be in control, so much so, that I lost control. I gave up my independence for dependency, chasing independence. WHERE THEY DO THAT AT?

How is it that I managed to misinterpret my given independence, and exchange it for a dependency that caused me to be subject to an outside source.

I had been fooled. But by who?

Who told me that I was not already independent? Why did I believe them? Where did I err? How can I be great and still afford my members to suffer under the subjection of my dependency?

It became apparent that until I take responsibility for my gift freedom, I will always be subject to the one who I blame for it not producing what I believe it should produce.

The great sovereign nation of America, makes every effort to be a beacon of light and defender of freedom in the eyes of the other nations of the world, but it proves, with staggering affirmation in the mental state of its inhabitants, to be at oft times, a hopeless abyss for many of its citizens. The spirit of apathy and complacency runs rampant through this great land of ours. We expect someone else to fix us, yet we miss the opportunity, time and time again, to be the change that we hope to see in our own community.

We protest everything and progress in nothing. We are as free as ever in body, but are held captive to the prevailing attitude of an enslaved mind.

We hide from our Damascus Road experiences that challenge us to make the adjustments necessary to be effective with the things that we have, as we long for the handouts that handicap us.

Let someone else do it. I don't want to do that.

We complain when we don't have what we feel we need and we get angry because no one has given it to us. We heard it was me against the world and then decided not to fight because we recalled that the world had already won the war against those who engaged it before us.

We had no one to teach us the art of war to ensure victory, so we must only be capable of defeat.

"The weapons of our warfare are not carnal, but are mighty through God to the pulling down of strongholds" 2 Corinthians 10:4

Where is my instructor to show me how to combat the enemy with purpose using these weapons that I have no knowledge of?

How can I defeat an enemy that I have no ideal of its tactics and capabilities, especially if I am diverting my fire power to a target that is not mission specific?

It's one thing to miss the target a time or two during the course of the fire fight, but it's a completely different matter when you've committed all of your resources to fight a war on the wrong front.

We assume the enemy is the other person we see with our two eyes. We are led to believe that our enemy is that person who caused us so much pain and anguish on whatever level that constituted a war of wills or a war of physical might.

Every time we engage in battle against someone who resides in the same house we damage the integrity of the home itself.

Oh what a tragedy, when the house has imploded upon itself. What grief must follow when the people of the house take account of the fact that they, in themselves, destroyed their home.

This debilitating condition of self sabotage, seems to be hereditary because I can recall, very clearly, my mother and father fell victim to this same condition. Come to think of it, I find it hard to recall any home that I frequented as a youth, that had not been ravaged by this condition.
I even thought I was immune to this disease, because of my self diagnosis and personally prescribed treatment for this condition. I figured that I had gave every consideration and determined a solution for this disease if it happened to show up in my life.

I WAS WRONG!

This condition overwhelmed me with such force that it was well after the divorce papers were served, had I realized that it was me tearing down the fragile walls of my relationship.

It was my persistence to strip my world according to my will, that exposed only my ignorance, in the wake of the destruction I had caused in the life of my ex-wife, and most disturbingly, my kids.

There is nothing to be added in division. There is no progress in oppression. There is no promise to be had when you sacrifice the purpose of why you are doing what you are doing.

The condition of self sabotage reaches even deeper to wreak havoc on the inside of you. Who declares war upon himself? The man who is a foreigner even to himself, declares war upon himself.

The level of ignorance, despair, and distress has to be at an unprecedented level when a man fails to acknowledge that it is on him to master himself.

It is his divine mission to live this life under the understanding that whatever obstacle he is to face externally, will also reveal an answer programmed in him internally, to overcome that obstacle.
There is NO TEMPTATION that will come to cause you to fall short of accomplishing this mission, that is not uncommon to any other man that lives on this earth.

It is the man who understands that his Maker is faithful to his design, in that He has considered everything, and placed an answer in you to address whatever you encounter.

This is the power that fuels your life and will also provide a way of escape, as necessary, so that you may be able to bear the load.

In life, you win the war based off of what you know. You lose the war because of what you don't know.

The army that is equipped with the full understanding of their capabilities is at an advantage. The army that also understands his adversary, in and out, will be guaranteed victory.

When we war internally, against ourselves, we commit suicide and save our real enemy the trouble of having to attack us in the first place. The real enemy has but to stand by and watch as we sabotage our gifts that have been given to us.

We fight with those we love in every area of our life. We war with our spouse. We engage in battle with our siblings and consider outright mortal combat against anyone who dares to oppose what we believe to be ours… BY RIGHT!

Not to mention after we have beat every one away from us, we turn the destruction inward as we tear at ourselves from the inside out with anxiety, self loathing, and depression. After we have fought, within the camp, we take the sword to ourselves, and resort to self-mutilation after we get the first look in the mirror at the person who just caused harm to those we truly loved. .

Understand this... the house you live in has the potential to reap exceedingly and abundantly above all that you can ever ask or think. It is not the number of people in the house that determines its effectiveness. In order for a house to be effective it must stand, in solidarity, as a house.

A house divided against itself cannot stand.

It is impossible for a half to wage war against a whole and expect to win, especially when the other half is fighting against it as well. The moment we allow division to rule in our lives we open the door for the enemy to simply walk in and lay claim to the land this house, as a whole, once stood on.

The war that is constantly causing casualty after casualty in your life is a war between two opposing worlds.

Don't get too far in space on me, because these worlds that war are actually fighting over and within you. The love that you were given to subdue the land is so powerful, that if it is not divinely ordered by the authority that gave it to you, you will most certainly KILL YOURSELF.

This power within is so strong that the thing that comes against you, can't defeat you unless you lay down in defeat.

Your enemy's world (kingdom, or rulers divine order) is in word only. He can only trick you to believe that you are not free.

The misuse and forfeiture of your independence can only be validated by your disobedience of your designed purpose. This is the flip side, and adhering to this flip side is guaranteed self destruction.

The noted singer/songwriter, Al Green, put it simply like this; 'Love will make you do wrong, and make you wanna do right'.

When you love through the ordination of your maker you will do right by His design. In contrary when you operate in a way that is contrary to your design, and seek to be independent above and apart from the intent of the One who made you, it will most certainly cause you to do wrong.

Webster defines independent this way.

> : not dependent: as
> *a (1)* : not subject to control by others : self governing *(2)* : not affiliated with a larger controlling unit <an *independent* bookstore>
> *b (1)* : not requiring or relying on something else : not contingent <an *independent* conclusion> *(2)* : not looking to others for one's opinions or for guidance in conduct *(3)* : not bound by or committed to a political party
> *c (1)* : not requiring or relying on others (as for care or livelihood) <*independent* of her parents> *(2)* : being enough to free one from the necessity of working for a living <a person of *independent* means>
> *d* : showing a desire for freedom <an *independent* manner>

We will use Newton's third law as a measuring stick as we examine this word. Newton's third law states, 'For every action, there is an equal and opposite reaction.' In laymen's terms, for everything you do, there is an equal and opposing force that is present, along with your action.

For our example of independent, we will change the verbiage in this law to say, 'For every pronouncement of your independence, there is an equal and opposite pronouncement of your independence.'

Plainly put, every time you declare, externally, or internally, your independence, there will be an equal (matching with force) and opposite (completely different doctrine) manifested concerning your declaration.

Seeing that you will make this declaration within yourself first, your declaration will be challenged, or meet its equal and opposite, within yourself. This is necessary to prove, even to you, the power of the belief you profess.

When you pronounce a positive affirmation in your life, according to the belief that you were made to be fruitful, to multiply, and to subdue the land; there will be an equal and opposite negative affirmation made to challenge your claim.
It is on you, what you believe after this negative is revealed.

Either you can see it as an indicator of the truth of your positive belief, or you can accept it as your new belief and dismiss the power of the One who afforded you the belief you held prior to.

Just know, when you give up your independence as a receiver and enter into a relationship as a giver, you will forever be expected to maintain that position, or your independence will become dependent and die. This false independence is a belief that you will have to make, shape, and mold. This type of independence will be unable to give to you, so hopefully you have enough in your treasure chest somewhere, to sustain your independence. This belief started with you giving so it must be sustained with your giving.

The world, or way of living, or kingdom, of your maker is your positive source. It will always lend to prosperity. It will always GIVE to your independence.

The world, or way of living, or kingdom, of the adversary is your negative source. It will always lend to lack. It will always TAKE from your independence.

You must give up something to take on the belief system of the adversary. That is not a true source. No one fills up their source. You draw from your source.

Be mindful that you are a creature, and your independence is subject to the parameters set by the creator. You can not fly on your own, as much as you can not scuba dive under your own power. You need the assistance of an outside interference to accomplish these tasks.

It is the fool who believes that there is no God. It is a bigger fool who has been blessed to ascertain their source and deny its power, in search of a power from their own efforts, that will never be suffice at completing the assigned mission.

How successful would a Marine be, if he set out to fight a war that was not ordained or funded by a higher authority?

Being a Marine myself, I would selfishly, and foolishly, make the statement that he would be very successful simply because he is a Marine, but the truth of adequate sourcing still remains.

That Marine's successful application of the power that was cultivated in him, is predicated upon his obedience, and cooperation with the collective forces that are purposed around him as allies.

As with any force of allies, they all fall under the overall guidance, and will of the Commanding Officer. If the Marine, does anything contrary to the C.O.'s will, he is considered a traitor and subject to being shot on the spot.

Insubordination does not equate to true independence.

There is a war of ideas and beliefs that is being waged in your life. As much as the outcome appears to be out of your control, you have been given the secret to victory on all fronts.

Obedience.

When you choose to operate in obedience to the design of your purpose, you will be able to stand and see the salvation of your Maker in every skirmish you find yourself in.

The Bible tells the story of Adam and Eve in the garden, encountering the temptation of the adversary. In this story, the adversary, in the form of a serpent, came to present the equal and opposite affirmation of independence to man.

The adversary challenged Adam and Eve's internal and external affirmation of freedom in the garden with the only power he had, his words. All the adversary could do was talk.

It was the responsibility of the independent man, when questioned to boldly approach the Maker when he began to reason, in himself, concerning his problem with the instructions. The adversary posed a question concerning the Maker, and Adam and Eve would have been better served, had they simply referred their concerns to the One who made the tree.

The simple solution would have been to say; "Hold on snake, let me ask God to be sure."

That question was not asked. Man took it upon himself to challenge the adversary in his own power and reasoned on the matter until the decision was made to eat the apple.

The interesting thing is, although it looked good to eat, the reason for them eating it was not to be filled, or sustained. The Maker said that they should eat fruit under the belief that it was food. They ate the fruit, under the belief that they would be exalted to a level of understanding, that turned out to be way above their pay grade.

Adam and Eve chose to make an independent decision and that was not the design of their independent gene.

Man's independent gene was designed to give him confidence to accomplish his mission, which was to be fruitful, multiply, and subdue the land. This gene was necessary to assure man that he was the responsible party and more than capable of accomplishing that task. It was when man decided to seek a mode of operation that was not conducive to his purpose, that the belief of his independence was altered.

When you choose to live independent, or free; you must be mindful of the choices you make, and the reasons you make them.

Your independence as a creature is linked to your obedience to your creator's design.

Don't be slack when you come against a force that challenges your belief in who you were called to be. The adversaries opposition is necessary. It is on you, as the independent creature, as to how you respond to this opposition.

I suggest you know the will of the world you were created to show forth, and not surrender your independence to the will of the world whose sole purpose is to announce the equal and opposite affirmation to the things that have been prepared for you.

Just because you meet an equal, opposite force doesn't mean you have come against a more powerful force. This force can not move you, save you surrender to be moved.

What the Maker has for you is for you. Fear not.

The one who has begun a good work in you, shall complete it. You will win this war. If only you believe.

Remember, you can not believe on what you don't know. You can't know unless you are taught. The teacher can't teach unless he be sent. He will not be sent unless the student is ready.

GET READY!!

When you know better you do better. Know who you are. Know where you are. Know where you are going. When you become a master of yourself you will walk confidently and know how, with the power that worketh in you, you can achieve, in every battle, a sweatless victory.

"The revolution is here, the revolution is here people. I said it once, I'll say it twice. You gots to be ready. The revolution is inside of you..." Talib Kweli

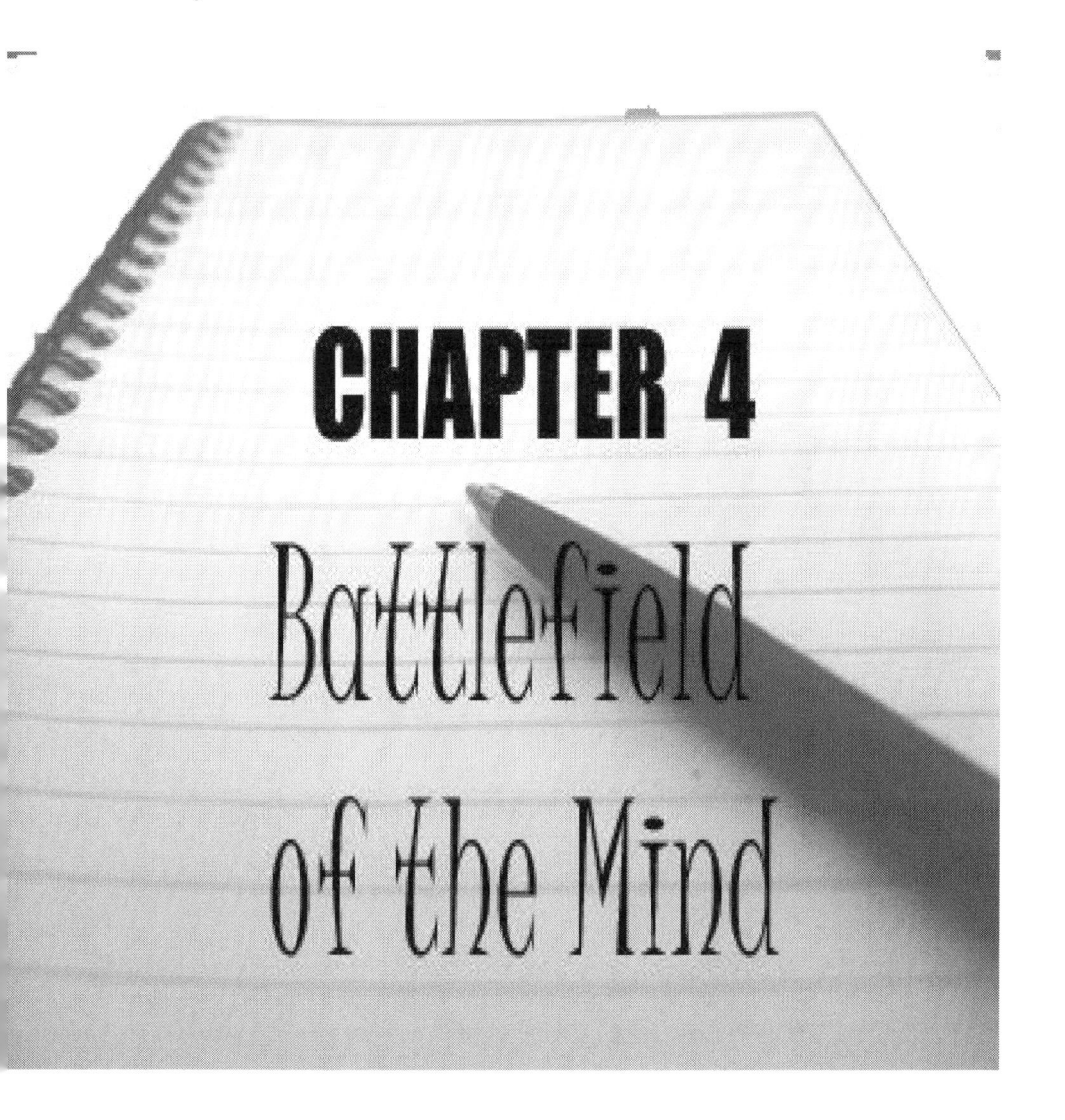

CHAPTER 4
Battlefield of the Mind

BATTLEFIELD OF THE MIND

What can I expect to face, now that I acknowledge that it is the integrity of my house that enables me to be effective in defense and resourceful in offense? If the person I see or the person I feel offended by is not my enemy then who is my enemy and where is this battlefield located?

You've been fighting all of your life, and unless you have been targeting the right enemy then your efforts have been in vain and often times, devastating to relationships that were never formed with division and destruction in mind.

Fighting on the wrong battlefield and against the wrong opponent, has proven to only strengthen the real enemy that you have yet to identify. This enemy lies in dark places, seeking, waiting for his opportunity to ambush you. He has studied you as long as you have been living with the sole purpose of bringing about your demise.

This enemy has invaded your most sacred place and has held siege to it while you wander aimlessly throughout your life, wondering why you're consumed with the facts of your failures. This enemy has, like a serpent, slid into the most inner parts of you and staked his claim to the battlefield so covertly, that you find it almost impossible to even accept yourself, that the place revealed as the true battlefield was even a battlefield at all.

This enemy is as real as Newton's 3rd Law is. This enemy has been tasked to be your equal, and opposite. The level that you aspire to reach, will present with it, an equal opposition that is necessary to prove your belief.

This enemy is not greater than your Maker.

This enemy is real, indeed, but his victory is never declared in your defeat. His victory is declared in your retreat.

If you resist this enemy, he will flee.

As we walk into this thought of the battlefield of the mind, I would like for you to consider every person that you would consider to be great. Now, arrange that list according to how intimate you are with their story.

For example, I consider my mother, my grandmother, Dr. King, Master P, and Jesus to be great. (to name a few). I would order my list according to intimacy, as Jesus, mother, grandmother, Dr. King, and Master P.

Begin to consider all of the things you would say they did great. Now, according to your level of intimacy with their story, compare that greatness, in consideration of the opposition you know they faced during that time their greatness was made manifest. You will see at work, an opposition that was equal to what their accomplishment was.

Know that to whom much is given, much is required. This opposition that you come against, may be strong but it does not have what you have. It does not have the purpose factor.

You are purposed to go where you are going. You are purposed to do what you believe you are supposed to do. You are purposed to have what you have. The only way you fail at achieving your purpose, is if you forfeit your purpose.

"For we wrestle not against flesh and blood, but against powers and principalities, and rulers in high places." Ephesians 6:12

I submit to you, that there is a place designated for battle, and that this place is occupied by you daily with submissive ignorance. In this place lies the only battlefield where warfare can be of any real effect, positive or negative, in your life.

This place is often times cluttered with the worries of the world. This battlefield is littered with concerns that range from the basic thought of what you will eat or what you will wear, to the more complex distractions like will my lights be on when I get home or will my significant other be there when I get home. In this place, the real struggle to discover who you are is muffled by issues that appear to be right now emergencies, but over time, all of these temporary issues fade into distant thoughts as the real unanswered questions eat at you like cancer, never to be addressed.

The war that is waged in this place, is oftentimes a one sided campaign where you lose before you can even muster a defense. This place is the only piece of real estate that you have an irrevocable deed to, but somehow you end up pawning it off to the enemy, like a title loan, for a temporary fix to these problems when he shows up roaring, as a lion, to bluff you into submission. This enemy waits ever so patiently, to call your loan into default when his temporary fix leaves you in what appears to be a bigger hole of debt.

Don't let the enemy repossess your inheritance. This place is your birthright, designed before the foundations of the earth, and purposed with prosperity. This place is where your understanding of all of this earthly experience is planted and nurtured, or ravaged with a vengeance like a plague of locust consuming a farmer's crops.

This place is the battlefield... the battlefield of your mind.

It is of utmost importance, to identify the battlefield because not only will you be engaging the enemy, you will be engaging the enemy within the confines of the terrain and topography of your mind. It then comes down to not who is the strongest or the fastest, but to who is the most knowledgeable at how to operate effectively in this terrain.

The victor will be the one who can assess the topography and strategically take the high ground in observation for defense, and navigate the valleys in combat on the offense. The conquering party will be the one who knows where every weak point is to either give it adequate support, or look to exploit it to gain entrance.

When you woke up this morning did you know that the negative things in your life search for breakpoints in your mind to make a sneak attack on your wellbeing? Did you know that the fear you have yet to identify is operating like a spy in your mind, passing on information to its allies that are gathering right under the nose of your ignorance, feeding them with information on how to breach the wall of your mind?

Every time you doubt the greatness inside of you, this spy sends a secret message to the enemy to let them know that what was once strong and unmovable, has been infected with the virus that fear has smuggled into your mind.

This virus weakens your defenses every time a loved one disappoints you. This virus spreads, like cancer, every time a bill comes due and you assess that you do not have the means to pay it. This virus, introduced by fear, will eat at you from the inside out. Its symptoms of depression and anxiety will cause you to let your guard down just enough so the main control room of your life can be overrun by the enemy. When this breach happens, the enemy will overload your system with every possible negative thought because he knows one thing you don't seem to know.

That one thing is this...

YOU REAP WHAT YOU SOW.

When you sow in fear, you reap in fear. Alternatively, when you sow in faith, you reap in faith. If the enemy can continue to rob you of your positive affirmations and replace them with the negative thoughts of how horrible and rough your life is, then he has taken control of the battlefield. If the enemy can get you to never take the time to study the deed of record for your life and realize that it already belongs to you, and that at any moment you can evict him from your land, then your ownership rights are of no effect. You don't even know you are the rightful owner. If the enemy can fill your head, in fear, with thoughts of doom and gloom, then it's just a matter of time before you surrender. He knows that... Do you?

"Watch your thoughts; they become words. Watch your words; they become actions. Watch your actions; they become habits. Watch your habits; they become character. Watch your character; it becomes your destiny." Lao Tse

Failure is not an option!

Victory is dependent upon YOU. You have been so equipped to win every battle that takes place in your mind.

The thing you must first accept, is that the pain you are experiencing is not because of someone else. These are your emotions that have run wild. These feelings of hurt and despair are allowed to continue, by you and you alone. You must take control of the battlefield in your mind. You must come to the understanding that EVERYTHING that happens in your life, can only have the emotional effect on you that you allow it to have.

You have been equipped, from the beginning of time to combat any opposition that should come against you in your life. We have been so blessed to live AFTER slavery. We have been blessed to live AFTER the civil rights movement. We have been blessed to break the chains of physical restraints. Now the true battle can begin. The battle for your mind.

I will be so bold as to announce your victory in the beginning if you make the choice to follow a very simple and strategic plan. This plan hung the stars in the sky and set the world on its axis. This simple plan walked down through time and showed the cave men how to make fire and the wheel. This plan set up, and set down kings on the earth, as it perfectly shaped a history that would be necessary to support its work in and through your life.

This plan I speak of is LOVE. If you grow to love, you will be privileged to go where love is going. If you make every effort to love your brother as yourself, your fort will be made so secure because when you turn on all the lights to show love, there is no place for darkness to exist in your kingdom. Your belief will be so strong that the very thought of the adversary will make you excited because it would be his opposition that prophesies to you, the level the Maker has in store for you.

You gotta love, My Nigga. At all cost, you gotta love. So learn to love. Love conquers all. Love is your weapon.

Why?

Because the opposite of love is what you believe to be coming against you. The hate and disdain of your opposition is weighing heavy on your heart, in the absence of your love. When you live with a love deficiency, your defenses are weak and it is easy for the enemy to come in and misdirect your power to keep you ignorant to the power of your love.

When the enemy is in control, every time your life requires love, the enemy will offer his substitute. This substitute is very attractive, and if you are not skilled in loving then you will accept his substitute. It feels like love… to you. It looks like love… to you.

You are led astray, ever so subtly, chasing after the lust of your flesh, the lust of your eyes, and the pride of life. Everything that is opposite to love becomes your quest when the situation arises.

When love is called upon to cover your spouse while they work out their understanding of life, you substitute it with your quest for personal gratification and demand that every need YOU have be met or else. When love calls on you to be longsuffering, as you are prepared for the next level of your life, you substitute love with your personal desire to have it now and you lust after it with reckless abandonment. When love calls for you to be humble because the greater good will be served by your service in the right spirit, you substitute it with a desire to be known of men, and allow the enemy to advance his attack further into your core, until you have no love in you, and the lusts have drained you of every reserve you had.

Learn to love, because lust needs no restraint. It has no control mechanism. When you give in to it, you are subject to wherever it leads.

Earlier we named some people who we considered great in some way or another. As you consider their greatness again, imagine them doing that great act out of a selfish lust, instead of the love that was so evident in their actions.

Do you think that Dr. King could have marched like he did if he was doing it for himself? Do you think Master P could have built his empire if he had not based his company on making something out of nothing for the ones he loved? Do you think Jesus would have took to the cross if it was all about what was in it for him?

Purpose must be defined in your life. Purpose will only be defined on the battlefield of your mind. It is on the battlefield where you will see the promise of your victory.

You must know that war is inevitable as long as there is an adversary. This adversary is equal, and opposite to you, like the New Orleans Saints Offense is to the Atlanta Falcons defense. There are 11 men on one side of the ball and 11 men on the other side of the ball. You must take the field to win. The rules don't allow 11 men on one side and 13 on the other. The opposition is always equal. Your victory is dependent upon your preparation and determination.

You play how you practice. Don't be surprised when you show up to a game, having not practiced, and you get blown away by the opposition.

I am struck with grief, when I think of the mind of My Niggas. My heart aches when I consider the many of us who struggle through this journey of life, unaware of the power that lies within us. We live in an age where technology is king and information is abundant.

A person can find many answers in the form of documented facts of history or published opinions of a respected scholar by simply typing in a query on any of the many online search engines. Yet, with so much perceived access sitting in plain sight, many of my brothers lay dormant in ignorance, as the enemy deceives them by playing on their misguided desire to be recognized by others as someone of merit.

Instead of being true to ourselves, we are led astray under the falsehood of public acceptance and the need to be affirmed by people who, in their own right, have no clue even who they really are or what they are purposed to do.

Talk about a tragic case of the blind leading the blind; one ignorant soul trying to convince another ignorant soul that their ignorance is more shinier than the other person's ignorance. They desire to put a new outfit and makeup on the fear that they are trying to hide. They try to dress up the fact that they have no clue who they really are.

Why else would they look for another person to validate their new car? Why would they buy clothes to make a fashion statement to those they want to impress? Why would they work tirelessly to win the camaraderie of others in hopes that they will be awed by what they have? What does it profit a man to gain the world, and lose his soul? War is being waged, in your mind, with or without your active participation. Your passive approach to this war only gives your enemy the latitude he needs to systematically break down your defenses and wreak havoc in your life.

The interesting thing about this attack is that it is not done in an attempt to conquer you and cause you to be submissive to his desires; The adversary does not want to hold you captive. This attack is launched with the sole purpose to seek and destroy. The adversary wants you DEAD.

The enemy you are up against does not want your talent. He is not concerned about your riches. The enemy wants but one thing; to eliminate the hope that lies in you.

He desires to sift you of all faith and convince you to fall on your own sword to make a mockery of the power that was placed in you, before the foundations of the earth.

He knows he can not defeat you if you resist him, so reasoning his war about getting your stuff is not his objective. You will actively resist him if you discover that he is after your stuff. The enemy's tactics are centered around convincing you, in fear, that either you don't have enough stuff or that you will lose the stuff you do have.

He offers solutions to this dilemma that are self oriented in nature because he knows your true power is made manifest when you are focused not on yourself, but on your purpose.
The enemy is well aware that the more you realize that 'Greater is He that is in you', the more you come to understand your ability to easily defeat him. When the enemy becomes your counsel then self destruction becomes the agenda.

" You see broke nigga racism, That's that 'Don't touch anything in the store'. And this rich nigga racism, that's that ' Come in please buy more. What you want, a Bentley, fur coat, a diamond chain?' All you blacks want all the same things. Used to only being niggas now everybody playing, Spending everything on Alexander Wang... New Slaves" Kanye West

CHAPTER 5
The New Slave Master

THE NEW SLAVE MASTER

In my laymen studies of slavery, I uncovered a covert control method that afforded the slave master with the power necessary to, with little to no physical restraints, control the lives of the early American slaves. This condition, I'm sure, is the control mechanism used to allow a few people, in any given area, to oversee, with little to no fear of an uprising, a multitude of human beings. This method was not only used during the institution of slavery, but shockingly, it is still being used during this current time today.

This condition I speak of, is the inability of the enslaved to maximize to their fullest potential, the power of their mind. If you can control the thoughts of a person, and cause him to consider only the things that render him a slave, and preoccupy his mind with only the accepted thought that his entire existence is predicated upon his ability to be a slave, then you can, with little to no effort, orchestrate the daily activities of that submissive slave.

"I'm broke." sounds the same as "I'z a slave." The self defeating statement, "I will never be able to own my own home." sounds very similar to "I'z never knows freedom."

It was only during the times that a slave intentionally thought, independently, from the thoughts of his slave master, that a rift between slave and slave master would occur.

Consider the Willie Lynch letter and the instructions this West Indies slave owner offered to its readers. If the slave master could preoccupy the slave with thoughts of dissension amongst themselves, and cause the slaves to internalize their hardship by acting out their disgust against each other, then the slave master becomes a savior, of sorts, that brings order and validation to their misguided thoughts of worth. Their desires for self worth would only be validated or denied by the slave master.

This puts the slave master in a very unique position, because the slave is, absent an inward compass, looking to affirm his existence outside of himself. He has unknowingly given himself up to be defined and directed by an outside power.

The power that provides for him is external. The power that instructs him is external. There is no awareness of the power within, so the physical can only manifest what the mind has accepted as truth. The slave acts as a slave because the slave believes, within himself, that he is a slave. He has substituted his power as a purposed being, with the ideals of an outside force.

MY NIGGA, SHAKE YOURSELF LOOSE!!!

Although we live in a time that proclaims, in word, that all men are free, I submit to you that this is not the case. The institution of slavery was legally abolished in 1865, but the spirit of slavery still reigns, with a heavy hand, in the lives of many people to this day, specifically in the lives of the African American.

The slave master has moved from the big house on the plantation, and has made his abode in the big house of the mind. When the physical chains of slavery were removed, the slave master of the mind was never served with the emancipation papers.

The slave was free in body, but was his mind free?

I am thankful for the opportunity to study the great minds of former slaves that announced freedom from the inside out, like Frederick Douglass and Booker T Washington, but you don't have to study their writings long to find that they too met face to face with 'free men' who were still slaves in their mind.

The movies we see today about slavery, does little justice in giving us a full picture of the mental makeup of the slave. When examining the writings of former slaves like Mr. Douglas or Mr Washington, you will discover stories of freed slaves who allowed their land that they possessed post slavery, to waste away for lack of proper cultivation. They substituted their responsibility to love freedom with their selfish desire to lust after freedom. They took no thought to progression and they chose to take pride in and make a big deal about the grandfather clock, or piano, that they had in their rundown shack of a home.

The free man, with no understanding of the personal responsibilities of freedom, often times, made every effort to distance himself from the work associated with slavery in exchange for the public perception of freedom. It was more important to the free man, to present himself free in his physical status, than to know himself free in his mind.

Couple this desire to appear free, with the many other unlearned, self-sustaining lessons that eluded the free man, and it's no wonder that it has taken over 150 years for the African American to stand truly, on his feet, as a free man.

Look at the slave before the 13th Amendment and compare him mentally, to the free man after the 13th Amendment. The male slave was often sold from plantation to plantation with no sense of responsibility to a family unit. There was no place for the male slave as a father in most cases and his position as a companion was often times reduced to being a stud for the growth of the masters slave population. At the least, he was expected to be a productive mule in the field.

The movies would have us to believe that the love between male and female slaves, somehow withstood the horrific nature of slavery. These movies would have us believe that at the abolishing of slavery, the male slave sought out his family that he had been separated from, and begin the next day, living in concert with the love of his life. The story would make every effort to leave us with the thought that these slaves went on to raise their children in a free and unrestricted world.

I would offer that this was not the case, or at least not the norm. The truth is, the female slave, if she still had her young child with her, most likely still depended upon the mercy of the slave master to establish a home for her children. The interaction between male and female as a unit was a task that had to be developed over time.

After the passing of the 13th Amendment, the limited resources available either restricted the movements of the free slaves, or caused them to travel abroad for some time searching for a place to call their home. The physical body was free, legally, but the mental makeup of the slave would, no doubt, take some time to adapt to establishing a social order that would be effective in raising the next generation of free African Americans.

What is the equal and opposite force to this plan you ask? These slaves had to pursue their purpose while only possessing the mental capacity of a slave.

So what we had, was a man who was mentally inept at being a progressive male figure in his community and a woman who was accustomed to making all the decisions concerning the house that she and her children resided in. These decisions were, of course, made with the slave master's overall purpose in mind. Her method of upbringing, was geared at rearing submissive slaves in spirit and resilient slaves in body.

If this was the conditions of the father who sired those before me, and the mother who raised those who went before me, I wonder how many changes in parenting had to occur to mold my mind today? I also question what hasn't changed, and what still remains as a crutch to my maturation as a free man today.

We can only look at the makeup of the African American family to see that this dysfunction has yet to be adequately addressed. The male slave was accustomed to not being an active member in his child's life, so unless he consciously made the decision to dismantle that thought in the minds of his children, he would, by his unconscious actions, pass that mental makeup down to his son. His absence would only amplify the misunderstanding of male/female relations in his daughter.

If this cycle was not broken, The male child would continue to experience the struggle between his free physical state and his oppressed mental state.

You see, unless there was an outside influence that awakened the free man in his mind, he would continue to fall victim to his thoughts of promiscuity and foster his apathy towards his offspring.

You are but a product of your environment. The key is to affect the change in the people's environment to affect the change in the people.

Fast forward to this age, and you can easily see this dysfunction still causing havoc in the African American community. We can explore this thought deeper and discuss the slave's mind in regards to 'the man', versus the free man's mind in regards to 'the man', but for the sake of not digressing too far, I will note that there is a familiar pattern that can be drawn between the mental dependency on 'the establishment' to provide for the WELFARE of the child, and the dependency of the slave female on the slave master's provisions to care for and raise her children in the absence of the father.

The ability to construct and maintain an environment that gives the child as much opportunity as possible is difficult, to say the least when you have determined that you have little to no provisions available.

Mental slavery is still alive and well in today's society and it keeps its stronghold by employing the same tactics that any other form of slavery would employ; keep the slave thinking about the oppression and dependent upon the oppressor.

In today's time, the minds of many of My Niggas are consumed with validating their freedom with stuff, and are oblivious to the responsibilities of being a free man in their mind. We have given up control of our ability to consider our purpose, to the slave master of our mind. This slave master wants nothing more than for us to waste away our existence chasing after the things of this world instead of being an impact on the progression of this world.

It is easier to just do what we know, than to entertain the prospect of those things we don't know. We know how to be a player. We know how to design our lives without concern for the next generation to follow. We know how to fight amongst ourselves and even kill each other over petty issues that have no weight on the overall goal of ensuring we leave an inheritance for our children's children.

Is it a mystery why many of us don't have a clue as to what our great grandparents names were? Many of our grandparents left us nothing with which to prescribe their name to. For many of us, the only thing we can attribute to our forefathers is our mindset. If they didn't pass down a free mind, I wonder what type of mind did they pass down?

Take solace, My Nigga, in the fact that there is a Father to us all, who still lives and looks to pass down to you, everything that has been withheld from you; If only you would believe and receive his instructions.

The ability to believe and receive this instruction was placed in you before the foundations of the earth. This gift was designated for you before any attempt to enslave you was ever considered. This awesome gift is so powerful that when you use even just a little bit of it, as much as the size of a mustard seed even, you can move mountains that exist in your life.

Where your biological father failed at showing you your gift in its fullness, I encourage you to seek the one who knew you before you were formed in your mother's womb. Inquire of Him to show you that gift on the inside of you that is more than capable to break the bonds of your mental slavery, and propel you to achieving greatness.

The first step to being set free is recognizing that you are not free, and knowing that you were made free. Whom the Son set free is truly free indeed.

Don't Worry. The Nigga Won't Read This.

"We can't change the world, unless we change ourselves."
Notorious B.I.G.

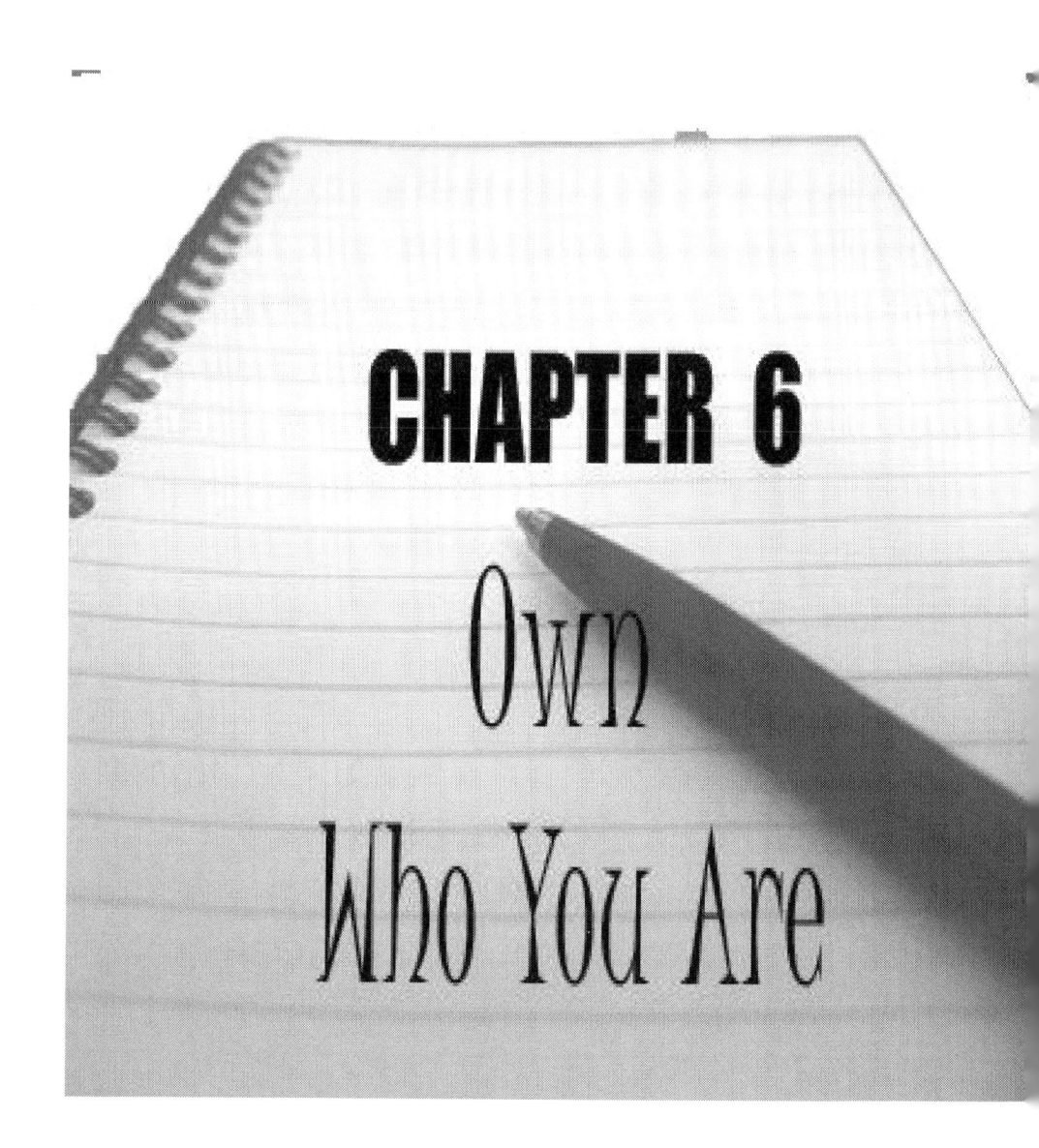

CHAPTER 6

Own Who You Are

OWN WHO YOU ARE

It is important to note in the onset of this chapter that you and I both will DIE! I make this announcement because it is in understanding this very truth that has propelled men to greatness, and it is the fear of this truth that has sent unfulfilled visions to the graveyard.

It was the fierce urgency of now that lead the march on Selma and set the stage for the revelation of a dream on the Washington Mall in 1963. It was the burning desire of change now, that fueled the actions of the 16th President of the United States, in his efforts to end slavery and end a war that was destroying all hope for the future to come after him. All things are made manifest in the fullness of time. This is your time…

How do you live knowing it's all leading to death? How can you, in good faith, build with everlasting intentions, something that will ultimately fade away?

Many questions run through my mind as I consider life. I question my existence in light of the fact that I am but 1 of billions of people on this earth at this very moment. I question the basic reasoning for my existence. I question my purpose and whether or not I even have purpose.

Living in this world for some years now, I believe, with a good level of certainty, that the socially professed purpose of life, often referred to as the AMERICAN DREAM, is the end goal many people around me would encourage me to live for.

It is accepted that in this capitalistic society, you would be falling on your sword if you didn't adopt the philosophy to own as much as you can and to do whatever you can to have the finer things in life.

This purpose sets owning your own home with a white picket fence, having 2.3 kids that attend private school while you commute to your comfortable 5 figure job, as its central focus and ideal end result. I admit that this is a very picturesque scenario, but what if that purpose doesn't line up with the purpose inside of you?

What do you do when you achieve the American Dream and still you feel the press of purpose rising up from the inside of your core, screaming at you with the fierce urgency of now?

What do you do when you gauge where you are and determine, in yourself, that you may never achieve the American Dream, yet the spirit of change stirs your inner man and you yearn to see the good things of the creation while in the land of the living?

Purpose gives everything its reason. Purpose expresses the intended design and ideal use of a person, place, thing, or idea. To understand purpose you must consult the manufacturer and get from him, in whatever form, proper instruction on how to effectively operate the creation.

How successful would you be if you attempted to toast your bread by placing it in the washing machine? Would you purchase a flat screen TV to use as a snow sled?

Imagine, if you will, that you were an IPhone 7. As you live this life as an IPhone 7, you have all of the emotions and feelings that you experience now. You have all of the advanced capabilities of an IPhone 7, yet everyday you wake up, make 2 phone calls, send out 1 text message, and spend the rest of the day hanging out with hammers trying to bang nails into a piece of wood. Every now and then you may hit the nail just right and get it to at least penetrate the wood, but more times than not, you end up with major scars and bruises and frequent visits to the repair shop to have your screen replaced.

You go home, empty, at the end of each day and consider all of the apps and the vast amount of accessibility you have via the internet, and vow that tomorrow you'll do better at being an IPhone 7.

Keeping in concert with every other day before, you find yourself with hammers banging away at nails until one day you pound on the nail and

Don't Worry. The Nigga Won't Read This.

it pierces through your casing and passes right through your motherboard. Your actions were contrary to your purpose, and in your selfish understanding, you destroyed all trace of the few phone calls and texts you did make.

Any potential you had to store gigabytes of information or process countless numbers of apps and programs is laid waste. The only story that is left to be told, is of the IPhone 7 who died, never running one app, and was found in the company of hammers with a nail through his motherboard.

It's a terrible sight to see when the creature has the latitude to decide whether to spend his time fulfilling his purpose, or to try and use his tangibles to affect a mission that he is obviously not equipped, or purposed to do, and he chooses the latter.

You are not an IPhone 7, but you are a creature who has been given the latitude to decide in what capacity, to make use of the awesome capability that you have been created and purposed to use.

The operative word in this scenario is creature. You are a creature, meaning, you have a creator.

Now I'm not one to be religious in any way, but looking at life objectively, from birth to death, it is obvious that we are created from something and we return to something. We understand, scientifically, that matter is neither created nor destroyed, so I submit to you that there has to be an outside force, outside of matter, that causes it to come together and take shape. Like the potter gathers the clay to form the bowl, your entire makeup has been gathered together and shaped for a purpose.

OWN IT.

Ownership is the ultimate manifestation of power. Everything owned is under the authority of its owner. The person who owns it will determine what is done with it. You desire ownership. This desire is apart of your DNA. When you own something, it is your discretion to do with it whatever you desire to do with it.

You may, at times, entertain the counsel of others, but in the end, you know, as owner, that you are at liberty to do with what you own, whatever you decide to do with it. What does it profit a man to gain something and not maximize the designed use of it? What good is it for him to own the rights to something and miss the sole purpose of having those rights in the first place?

You have been given ownership rights to your life and it is ultimately on you to exercise those rights.

OWN YOUR PAST.

In owning and understanding your past you will find a peace that will sustain you in your today, and a hope that will propel you into your tomorrow. You must accept everything that happened as fact and resolve to see it work together for your good.

It is the negative feeling of not being where you feel you are purposed to be that will move you to do those things that will get you moving in the direction that you know you are supposed to be going in. So, in this instance, your negative was necessary for direction.

As a people, we must accept that slavery was necessary for the greater good and find in it the motivators necessary to move in the direction we are destined to move in. We must own the fact that our male figures are scarce in our community and use it to motivate us to fill the void that has snared most of us along the way. This void has consumed many that failed to escape its black hole-like pull.

We must learn to listen to our inner man that knocks patiently at the door of our hearts, waiting for the moment we open the door and let it come in to instruct us in the way.

You may not know how you are supposed to be great, you just first need to know that you were made to be great.

Each time you find yourself in a place where you recognize that you are not operating according to the potential you feel you are capable of operating at, you must take the time to seek out your maker to learn, with certainty, your purpose. You must come to the understanding of how to affect your purpose with the capabilities you were made with. Let's look at the IPhone 7 scenario again. Now, instead of trying to own the life of a hammer as his own, the IPhone 7 has decided to own the fact that he is an I Phone 7. He has come to the understanding that he is capable of so much more by getting around other IPhone 7s that were doing all kinds of awesome things. Every time he saw another IPhone 7 in action something inside of him rose up and he longed to do those things he saw other phones do.

One day when he was searching inside himself, he stumbled across a website that had the full operators manual on how to be an I Phone 7. He read as much as he could of that manual as often as he could read it. The IPhone 7 began to do as much as he could, in his own understanding, all that he learned from reading the manual.

Wanting to know more, the IPhone 7 decided to call the manufacturer and inquire of him, about this one program he could not quite figure out.

While on the phone with the manufacturer, the IPhone 7 discovered that the manufacturer had a 24/7 technical support line specifically designated for him, and that he is encouraged to call on the manufacturer as often as he can to get real time support and time sensitive upgrades to ensure he runs at his max capacity. The IPhone 7 called the line every day and every day he learned to operate, with a great degree of mastery, according to his intended purpose.

The IPhone 7 found his true purpose by understanding that he was purposefully created. He took joy in his decision to seek the manufacturer's wisdom in effectively operating in the purpose, that lead him to maximize his uniquely designed capabilities. Now, with the story of the IPhone 7 ending with mastery; consider your life as this IPhone 7.

OWN WHO YOU ARE.

The most damning thing I see in My Niggas, is that most of us don't own who we are.

I will take this time to say that although I use the word nigga as a label, I am in no way submitting to the context of being "just a nigga". If it is not apparent up unto this point, my use of the word nigga is in the same spirit as saying "my brother". I choose to use this word because I really want 'my brother' to keep reading and know that I am writing this for him.

I know there will be people who read this book and find offense in my use of the word but it is my belief that just as natural as we have owned the word 'nigga' that was placed on us, we can own the purpose that was placed in us. Each and every one of you were made for such a time as this.

Inside of you has been gathered a unique set of talents and abilities, that when properly applied, will make that everlasting impact on the world to come. When you own who you are, and learn how to operate according to your creators intended purpose, you will be effective.

You must own who you are.

It is your mission to discover all of the greatness that lies within you. No one will pull your greatness out of you. You will have opposition, but it is your purpose to manifest your greatness. Each of us have been given a unique set of skills to affect a very unique purpose. None of us are alike. Understand that it is on you to be fruitful, multiply, and subdue the land.
Become a student, that studies to show himself approved in his work. Learn to rightly discern and implement the strategy that is given to you. The hope that you have to be the conduit for the prosperity of your

children's children, is dependent upon your willingness to be filled with your purpose.

Own who you are and not who others say you should be.

You must take your place under the flow of your source, and be filled with the provision appointed just for you. Don't get sidetracked trying to take ownership of something you see in someone else's cup. What is deposited in their cup is for them. What is deposited into your cup is for you.

When you learn to own who you are, you will find that as you command YOUR place under the flow, you will be filled to the point of overflowing. It is from this overflow that all the giving you will ever give will come from.

There is no need to take it upon yourself to fill someone else's cup. As the Maker allows, He will position those whom he pleases under your flow. This appointment is made with eternity in mind. So if you are not in position to overflow, don't be surprised when you have no one gleaning from your experience with the Maker.

Imagine that there is a pyramid of champagne glasses stacked strategically on the table. As you begin to pour champagne into the top glass, it fills and overflows into the receptacles of the glasses below them. The more champagne you pour into the top glass, the more the overflow fills the glasses below. Take notice that if any of these glasses get out of position, there will most definitely be champagne spilled all over the table.
Picture in your mind, the top glass taking it upon himself to bend over and pour its contents out into the glasses below him.

As I'm sure you imagined, not only will he interrupt the flow, but he will empty out his supply rather quickly and be of no effect. The source has been cut off and the top glass has to figure out, in himself, how to get back in position to be filled again, save the pourer has mercy and redeems the glass to its original position.

You are that champagne glass. You have been strategically placed to receive according to the Maker's divine order. When He pours into you, all you have to do is be still and be filled. You don't have to bend over and you don't have to empty yourself out. As He fills you, just stand.

After you've done all you can to stand... keep standing. In the fullness of time, you will be filled and your cup will overflow. Every desire you have to fill your children with the truth of purpose will be met as the overflow runs down into their cup. They will learn, by watching you be still, so when it is there time to be filled, they will know in observation, and in practice, to be still and let the pourer do his thing.

You were chosen to be apart of this flow. You were called to stand in this time. This is your hour to exercise your faith in the one who made you. He wants to fill you up and overflow down into generations to come.

Own who you are.

When you own who you are, you establish an inheritance to pass down to your children's children.
The fullness of time has come for you to set aside every obstacle in your life that, so easily, hinders you from being who you believe you are to be. The bonds of mental slavery have been broken, and now is the time for you to seek out your true purpose and live out your destiny. You no longer have to live out the purpose prescribed to you by the people in your life.

You are not just a nigga. You are not just a drug dealer. You are not a deadbeat dad. You are not an unfaithful companion. You are not broke. You are not hopeless. You are not oppressed.

You are a man who will live with integrity and at peace with all other men. You are a father who will press to establish an inheritance for your children's children. You are a friend who will love his neighbor as you love yourself. You are a business owner who will develop a new way to do business . You are a professional who will take your trade to the next level. You are the inventor who will design the next great wonder of the 21st Century. You are a purposed creature that has been designed to do exceedingly and abundantly, above all that has been imagined up unto this point. You are free to be who you know, in yourself that you are.

OWN IT.

"I know what it means to fall off, and gotta come up from nothing... but I steady be hustling, on top, gotta stack me some change, but who's to blame? If I came here rich, would it ever have been the same" Block Boi

CHAPTER 7
Own Where You Are

OWN WHERE YOU ARE

Where you are is real. Don't fool yourself. Life, up unto this point, has happened. No matter how 'good' or 'bad' life has been to you, it is where you are that matters the most. You must own where you are.

Remember when you own it, you have the ultimate say on what's done with it.

It is imperative, at this point, that you understand that where you are, is what you own and what you own is what you have to work with.

I'm not suggesting you own it with the intent of staying in that state forever, I am saying own it so you can know that because you own it you can do with it what you want to do with it.

So if you find yourself in the home of a depressed person... OWN IT. There have been many plots of land that held the home of a depressed man that have been remodeled to be the homes of successful CEOs.

If you find yourself in the home of a convicted felon... OWN IT. I personally know scores of felon properties that have been rehabbed to be the homes of successful business owners.

It is still your property to do with it what you feel. You can either let it sit idle, with no attempts at upkeep, in the ghetto of life, or you can begin the renovation process that not only increases the value of your home, but consequently, your renovation process has the potential to spark the renovation of other homes around you.

Everything about your life has been so designed to prepare you to fulfill your purpose. It is not wise to dismiss any aspect of your life as insignificant because every time you find yourself under the weight of your situation, you are presented with the opportunity to grow stronger and build the muscles necessary to be effective in your purpose.

Life is one big workout routine. It amazes me how similar the act of building your physical muscle runs in the same vein as the act of building your mental muscle. Neither one of these muscles will grow strong if they are not submitted to the opposition of an opposing force.

Even if a person does not actively participate in a physical workout program, by simply engaging in motion to do the daily everyday tasks that they commit themselves to, they are engaging, on some level, an opposition while going about those tasks.

Gravity presents the necessary opposition for physically moving about this earth. It is gravity that opposes and causes the baby to use its arms to push against the weight of his body to raise up and physically engage with the world around him. Every time that baby wants something that is not in his hands, he will begin to engage every muscle he owns until he determines, in himself, the adequate combination of muscles, in resistance to gravity, that is necessary to get to whatever he has in mind to get to.

It is not until he has given up on this exercise does he cry out for help. Over time, the will (purpose) of the baby, takes him through his workout routine until he masters on some level, the ability to raise up and crawl, stand up and walk, and ultimately lean forward and run.

It is a natural reaction for you to consider, in yourself, ways to achieve your desired result. Like the baby, you must take the time to own every muscle in your mental body, and work them out in tandem with each other, until you find the right combination to achieve your desired result.

Unfortunately, over time, our resolve is weakened when we don't get what we believe we should have, and fall back on our childish impulse to give up and cry out for someone else to come along and give us what we want. As we grow into adulthood, we hold on to our safety valve of immaturity, out of fear that we may not be able to do the thing we set out to do.

The greater the level of commitment, seems to present with it, a greater level of opposition and the baby in us cries out for help, pushing the great man in us into exile. These moments of opposition are ordained and specifically designed to workout the great man inside of you. It is childish to expect to be able to get to where you want to be, without having to do any work to get there.

"When I was a child, I spake as a child, I understood as a child, I thought as a child, but when I became a man, I put away childish things." 1 Corinthians 13:11

Within the boundaries of the internal real estate that you own, lies everything you need to accomplish your purpose. You own every resource that is necessary to push you to your destined end result.

The key that opens the door to this storage facility is understanding. Your creator has designed this lock to be opened only by the person who has took the time to know that the resources that are housed in this storage area are to be used only for the fulfillment of your purpose.

It is important that you understand what your purpose is because even after you obtain access to this storage area, you can not use one tool effectively. You must not only possess the faith that the tool is able to do the job it was designated to do, but also the faith that you are qualified and competent to use the tool, with precision, to accomplish the task.

It is not wise to take a chainsaw and use it as a blender to mix cake batter. You might get the mix to turn over somewhat, but if you truly engage this tool in mixing cake batter, you can expect to splatter the mix everywhere and you run the risk of ruining the bowl you are mixing in. Not to mention, the threat of physical harm you introduce to yourself in your foolish attempt to use a chainsaw as a cake batter mixer.

This is the way many of us approach our mental property. We have spent the formative years looking for the easy way to decorate our space, and desired the things that clutter and distract us from actually accomplishing the mission that burns, like fire, on the inside of us.

We have allowed this clutter to drown out that fire, and if asked, many of us can not adequately define our own personal mission statement in life because this clutter has handicapped our understanding.

Is it strange to you, how easy it was in the early stages of our formative years to tell anyone who asked, about our goals and ambitions? But as the older we got and the more we determined the level of work required to achieve that goal, we lost the definition we held concerning that goal and faded to obscurity in our understanding of what it was that we were living to accomplish?

"To whom much is given, much is required..." Luke 12:48a

We want much, but we do not want to do much.

As adults, we are consumed with the 'needs of existence' and we have abandoned the pursuit of our purpose. We feel, inside of us, the pull for greatness but we dismiss it, shamefully, in the face of our temporary need.

I often ponder the questions:
Why would a creator, who has made His power evident in the complexity of the design of his creation, not provide the tools necessary for the creature to be completely effective in its purpose?
Why would the Creator allow the worries of existence, to suffocate the aspirations of his progressive minded creation? Why do I have a crying mechanism if I am expected to do all things in my own strength?

We only have to look at the complexity of the human body to understand that it's complicated design, allows for it to be adaptive to the most extreme conditions presented in this world. The ability of the body to sustain itself by self regulation is a testament to the awesome mind of the creator.

It is this same creator, who has so shaped you to be effective in the environment that you find yourself in. Whatever it is that you need to accomplish your purpose, your creator has provided, within you, the things necessary to improvise, adapt, and overcome. All of this that can be done, will be but a testament to the creativity of the creator to make a creation that has the ability to assess a situation and cause the response for overcoming it to manifest from within itself.

So when you are faced with the threat of not being able to pay your light bill, inside of you is the process necessary to address that obstacle, because it is a need that is required to afford you the opportunity to achieve your purpose.

Understand this, you can not access the process that is necessary to address this matter, unless you are clear, in faith, of the reason that obstacle must be removed. If you are not clear of your purpose, removing that obstacle will be all but impossible.

It is childish to assume that removing this obstacle is necessary to make sure your kids have a home with lights. That is a temporary thing because eventually your kids will be out of that house. This approach is like crying for someone to move you from the position you put yourself in, and unless you understand the purpose of that obstacle in relation to your purpose, you will find yourself back at that obstacle again and again.

You must own who you are as a man and put away childish things. Your crying mechanism should mature to an inquiring mechanism that seeks to know and understand the reason an obstacle is standing in your way. You must come to terms with the fact that the obstacle is presented to make you stronger in light of your purpose. It is imperative that you inquire of the maker for solutions and refrain from crying out in hopes that somebody, anybody, will hear you.

A man makes his moves on purpose. That is why you are legally held responsible for breaking the law even if you are not aware of the law.

Ignorance of the law does not free you from the punishment of breaking the law. Ignorance of the process does not free you from the consequences associated with trying to manipulate the process.

When you were a child it was expected that you cry out in a childish way. It was expected that you perceive everything that happened to oppose you in doing what you were tasked to do, as someone else's fault. It is childish to expect someone else to correct what you, in your ignorance, messed up.

As a man, you must put away childish things. You must own every aspect of where you are. You must own the fact that even if someone comes up and punches you in your face, it was on you to be aware and find the process necessary to avoid that action or be subject to getting punched in your face again.

Finding fault is childish. Owning where you are and working on it until you achieve your desired result, is being a man.

You are capable of doing just what you set out to do, if it lines up with your purpose.

There is no provision made for you, outside of your purpose. Seeking these things is a waste of resources, and you must become wise in the use of your resources, because there may come a time when the resource you expended chasing those things that were outside of your purpose, could have been used to easily overcome an obstacle that is in the way of you winning the race you were assigned to run.

No, it is not over if you come across an obstacle that requires a process that has been weakened by misuse. You only have to be patient in strengthening that process through proper instruction from the creator to get back on the road, racing toward the finish line.

Take confidence in knowing that the race that you are running, is not given to the swift nor to the strong, but to the one who endures until the end.

Don't Worry. The Nigga Won't Read This.

"I'm not a businessman... I'm a business, man." Jay-Z

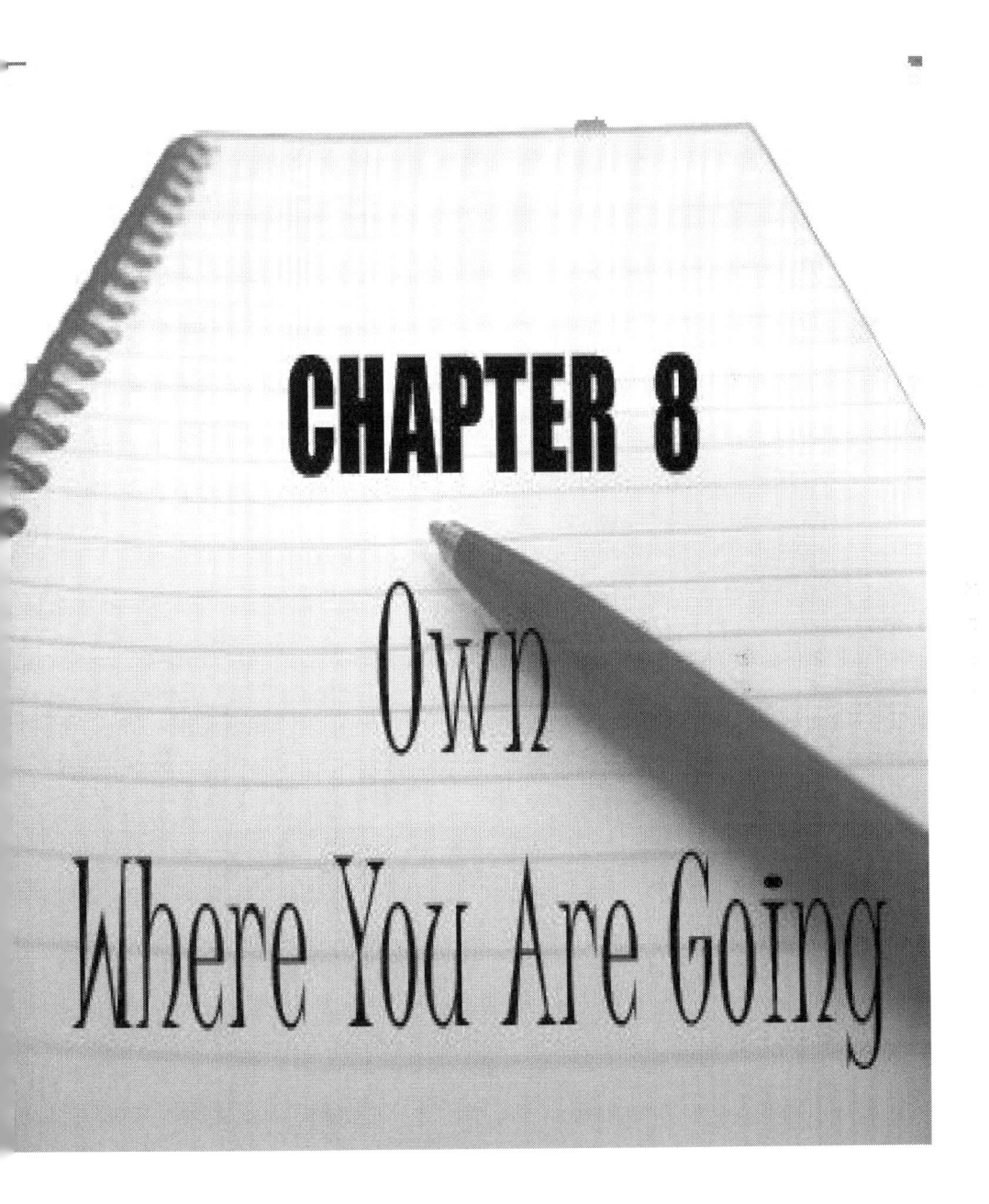

CHAPTER 8

Own Where You Are Going

Don't Worry. The Nigga Won't Read This.

OWN WHERE YOU ARE GOING

The past 30 years are a prime example of the spirit of progression manifesting itself in the lives of the inhabitants of this great country.

We have moved from talking on a landline phone connected to a long wire that ran throughout the house, to cell phones that also serve as personal computers.

We have seen advancements in medicine that are constantly achieving new heights in the understanding of wellness and repair of the human body. Major barriers that hindered the progression of our social makeup have been challenged and many of them torn down, to make way for ALL MEN to live in a land, free, with certain inalienable rights that were endowed to him by his creator.

We can name countless number of advancements that show forth the awesome prowess of human ingenuity, but I will focus on the one that has been the most influential in the African American community, specifically those in the community that are 40 yrs old and younger, to highlight the potential that exists in each and every person that has, in some way, felt the sting of past and present oppression.

This advancement, I speak of, is the progression of HIP HOP as an industry. Hip Hop progressed from the side streets and basements of the inner city, to being, arguably, the most influential musical genre across the globe. Hip Hop mimicked its founders in every aspect in the beginning and it showed the execution of purpose in its leaders as it grew into a multi-billion dollar industry.
At its inception, Hip Hop was considered a fad, at most. This perception of Hip Hop was held by white and black people alike.

The fervent expression of raw emotion, sampled over the classic LP's of these youth's parents, was dismissed as gibberish and rebellious. To actually tell the story of the ghetto with no sugar coating was offensive to many, but it was just what the artists had in mind. It was just what the listener needed, to bring a sense of awareness to the struggle to just 'make it', that the listener was experiencing.

The entire movement took off because of the necessity of purpose to tell their story, their way... uncut.

They wanted to own their expression and opposed the naysayers with a resolve that produced the soundtrack and paved the road to a revolution that would not be televised.

This revolution spread across the country because its call woke up the sleeping giant in a generation that wanted more, but had only a few examples of how to get more.

The lyrics of these pioneers spoke to what most of the youth of the African American community were feeling and experiencing after the end of the Civil Rights movement. It spoke of the struggle necessary to adjust, as a community, to live integrated in a system that prior to that time, had spent its entire existence as a segregated system.

These youth were free in body, free to go to public schools with whites, but struggled still with the desire to achieve the American Dream. Their communities were in decline, drug use ravaged the social security of their community and black on black crime was nurtured by the misguided desires to present freedom in material possessions. The struggle intensified while the understanding of freedom was never taught.

Hip Hop was the expression of wanting more out of life than where you were. Hip Hop faced the same type of opposition you may face today... Hope with no tangible resources.

HIP HOP also had the same thing you have today... PURPOSE.

What made Hip Hop great was its unrelenting push to make of itself, what it believed it was designed to be, and not just what it heard it should be.

The pioneers of Hip Hop were drug dealers and pimps. The pioneers of Hip Hop were sons and daughters raised in single parent homes. Hip Hop was served with utility shut off notices and was evicted several times from the mainstream of American acceptance.

Fast forward 30 years and the one lesson I would have you to learn is this:
Hip Hop never gave up.

OWN WHERE YOU ARE GOING.

The resolve to not be denied your purpose has to initiate and rise up from the same place that a clear definition of your purpose must be defined; from within.

You must own where you are going, despite the obstacles you see standing in your way.

We have discovered earlier in this book, that ownership is the key to achieving your purpose. You must own every aspect of who you are. You must own every aspect of where you are. You must own every aspect of where you are going.

The person who owns it has the final authority to say what is done with it. In order to get where you believe you are supposed to go, you must own every aspect of the journey.

Owning where you are going is similar to taking a road trip.

The person who decides to take a road trip must first own his planning process. The one who takes ownership of the planning of the trip, must consider, in detail, every potential change and adjustment that can happen during the trip. The planner must consider the day of departure, the mode of transportation, the provisions necessary to sustain the trip, and the events that will take place upon arrival.

It is not wise to take off from Gulfport, MS in route to Atlanta, GA with no provision made for refueling during the trip.

No three day trip should be made without ensuring you have packed 3 days worth of provisions or have put in place another well orchestrated plan to ensure the provisions are met upon arrival.

I would submit to you, that when you plan your trip in life, you must take the necessary time to own your planning process.

After the plan is in place, the owner of this plan must oversee, with careful observation, the execution of this plan. It is feasible to delegate many tasks necessary to make this trip, but the oversight of the execution of that delegated task, must be done by the owner.

A road trip must have a qualified driver that is capable of operating the mode of transportation from the starting point to the end destination. Adequate lodging must be arranged to ensure the participants are as comfortable as possible during the trip.

If the family is going to Disney World, it would be wise to ensure there is lodging that would lend to the family feeling comfortable during the trip and allowed the opportunity to focus on enjoying the park. A responsible planner would make every effort to make sure his party is not preoccupied with the thought of where they will lay their head. During the execution of this plan, there must be an owner who oversees the process throughout the trip.

When you own where you are going, you have the ownership rights, and responsibility to cause everything within your disposal, to come into play to achieve the purpose set forth during the planning process.

If you claim ownership to life as a doctor, you must cause everything you own to line up with your designated purpose of being a doctor.

Remember, you can only cause what you own to line up with your purpose. So if you don't own what you determine you need, you must use what you do own to get what you determine you need to accomplish your desired end result.

If you need money for school, you must seek out opportunities to trade off the things you do own, like the ability to apply for financial aid and grants, to take ownership of the money needed to enroll in school. If you don't have the grades necessary to get admission into the school of your choice, you must make whatever adjustments you can to bring your grades up to par, or at the least, research another institution that is better fit to respond to the things you do own.

The pioneers of Hip Hop didn't have a major distribution deal. The pioneers of Hip Hop were, most of the time, denied the opportunity to sign to major record labels. The pioneers of Hip Hop were denied the radio play necessary to get their music out on the air waves during its infancy.

But understand this, the pioneers of Hip Hop had a level of determination that looked these obstacles in the face, owned the fact that they were there, and went to work to find a way to overcome every obstacle.

Every effort was made to overcome the barriers that hindered Hip Hop's progression to become the industry that would eventually make it possible for many recording artists, producers, promoters, managers, image consultants, bloggers, and other supporting cast members, to provide a very comfortable and progressive lifestyle for themselves.

The ends do justify the means. You must first determine that your means will be initiated only in the implementation of your purpose.

If you determine, in studying your purpose, that every resource at your disposal, and every obstacle that lies in your way, is under your control, then you will be able to put every positive and negative in its proper place to affect your purpose.

We live in a time where overt oppression is frowned upon to the extent that it is determined to be illegal if the oppression comes to deny you from experiencing your God-given rights of life, liberty, and the pursuit of happiness.

I submit to you, that we waste valuable time stressing over a perceived oppression and we miss the opportunity to stave off the attack of the real oppression that is keeping us from seeing our purpose made manifest.

When you waste your energy fighting against an already defeated foe, you give the defeated life just enough, that you trick yourself to believe that it is still a threat worthy of focus . All the while, the real enemy sneaks in, ever so slyly, to cloud your sense of direction.

When you fall victim to this trickery, it will cause you to wander around aimlessly for years, at an obstacle that you were well equipped to overcome in a matter of minutes. This sleight of hand, is the most effective tactic of the enemy because if he can keep you preoccupied with a dead issue, he can keep you from pursuing a live purpose.

You only have one life to live.

This truth is best proclaimed by the acronym YOLO... You Only Live Once. When you accept the fact that you only have one life to achieve your purpose then you will begin to put into perspective the full scope of your purpose and not allow time to be wasted engaging a task that is taking away from achieving that goal.

Most of the obstacles you encounter can easily be overcome by simply sidestepping the issue and not looking back. When you look back at a small issue, you take your eyes off of where you are going and run the risk of crashing into an obstacle that is in front of you. The risk of this upcoming crash can not be measured until it happens.

You don't know if it will just be a fender bender, if it will total out your vehicle, or if it will be the crash that ends your life. Taking your eyes off the road ahead and focusing on the obstacles in the rear, can end your life.

Where you are going affects those who are to come after you. Your kids will be affected by where you are going. Your significant other will be affected by where you are going. Your family and friends will be affected by where you are going. You will be affected by where you are going. If you are to achieve your desired result, you must own it and make every move necessary to ensure that what you own lines up with the intent of its owner.

What happened in the past is over. No matter how much time and effort you put into changing that event, you will never change what has already happened.

What is happening now is happening.

This is where you are allowed the liberty to make adjustments. Right now is the time to make whatever changes necessary, to set you on course to achieve the future you have claimed ownership of.

Doing the same thing and expecting different results is considered insanity. Are you insane?

I believe that if you have read this book up to this point, that you are far from insane. The only thing left to do now is to make the adjustment. Do something different.

If you have tried complaining for years and nothing has changed, try humbling yourself, and look for solutions to solve the problem versus making a fuss about the fact that you have a problem.

If confrontation has been your mode of operation, try walking away and dismissing the opposition by owning the fact that you are on course.

Any energy you give to this temporary distraction will be unavailable when you need it at the next workout station you encounter along the way.

The Bible speaks of sin as the thing that keeps a person from being effective in their designed purpose.

When studying this word sin, I found that it was an archery term that simply meant ' to miss the mark'.

During earlier times when archery was a very popular sport, the archer would shoot an arrow at the target and if he missed the target, the spotter would yell 'SIN'. Upon this announcement, the archer would consider all of the things that were in his control and how they could affect his shot, and made whatever adjustments that were necessary to accurately affect the target.

Yes he had 'sinned', but if the archer did not make the required adjustments, then he would continue to miss the target.

The penalty for continuing to miss the target, would amount to the archer being without the necessary points needed to win the tournament.

This is the case with your life.

As you own where you are going, there will be times when you 'sin' along the way and miss the mark. It is of the utmost importance, that you take the time to make the necessary adjustments within yourself, and better use the resources that you are employing to hit the mark of your purpose.

Do not take this journey being stubborn, and refuse to make the adjustments that must be made to get you to where you believe you are supposed to be. Life is full of lessons to be learned, and if learning the lesson is a must to pass on to the next objective, then you must be prepared to make the adjustment to learn the lesson along the way.

Remember YOLO.

In this one life that you are living, the sky is truly the limit. All other limitations are self imposed, or self allowed.

Either you place the limitation or you allow the limitation imposed on you by others, to remain.

When you own where you are going, you have the authority to speak even to the biggest mountain that stands in your way, and tell it to be removed.

YOLO.

Own where you are going.

Don't Worry. The Nigga Won't Read This.

"Now faith is the substance of things hoped for, and the evidence of things not seen." Hebrews 11:1

CHAPTER 9

NOW Faith is

NOW FAITH IS…

I have faith in the purpose inside of you. I have hope in the thing that has yet to be revealed from inside of you.

There are buildings that have yet to be built. There are songs that have yet to be sung. There are books that have yet to be written. There are business ideas that have yet to be set in motion. There are inventions that have yet to be made.

All of these things, I believe in faith, will be made manifest, as we come to the understanding that we must own who we are, where we are, and where we are going.

This journey called life, has been set up as such, to respond, in kind, only to your purpose. Any effort made outside of your purpose will bring confusion that if not addressed, will systematically incapacitate you and prevent you from arriving at your desired end.

Your life is not to be left to chance.

Your life was designed with purpose, and unless you search, within yourself to define this purpose, you will continue to spin your wheels while you grow in despair, as others pass you by.

There is no one to fault for who you are. There is no one to fault for where you are. There is no one to fault for where you are going.

All of the obstacles you encounter along the way, have been uniquely designed to work together for the good of you achieving your purpose. In you, My Nigga, lie the answers needed to address the daily dilemmas that you face. You do not have to submit to what 'they' say you are. You do not have to live where 'they' say you should live. You do not have to go where 'they' say you should go.

You are the master of your domain. You are the captain of your ship. You are a Champion. You are a Winner. You are the Best of the Best.

It is my desire, as you come to the end of this book, that you are empowered to actively make the adjustments necessary to effectively hit the mark you feel you are purposed to hit.

No matter what stands in your way, there lies in you, the ingenuity to improvise, adapt, and overcome.

No weapon formed against you shall prosper, when you tap into the power that lies within you. Your power source is able to do exceedingly and abundantly above all that you can ask or think could happen. You were made for such a time as this.

This is your time.

Your purpose required you to be born the descendant of a slave. Your purpose required you to be raised in a single family home. Your purpose required you to learn the lessons of a felon. Your purpose required you to overcome addiction. Your purpose required you to love when your natural reaction was to hate. To whom much is given, much is required.

When you overcome these obstacles not only will you be liberated, but you will set the example for those who have been given the opportunity to bear witness to your triumph.

Your testimony just may compel them to push past the opposition in their lives.

This is why I wrote this book. I wrote this book because I believe in you, My Nigga.

I know that you becoming an overcomer, is as important to me and my lineage, as me being an overcomer is to you and your lineage. We have been blessed to share this lifetime together and I pray that we never give up and faint not, in anticipation of seeing the goodness of the Lord in the land of the living.

Eyes have not seen, ears have not heard, neither has it entered into the hearts of man, the things the creator has in store for those who decide to live out their purpose.

There will be many obstacles along the way. Small and great obstacles will be encountered as you travel the road of purpose. You must know, as you take this journey, that in you lies everything you need to get to the place you are destined to be.

I beseech you, my nigga, to be strong in the power of your creator because it is with that power that you were made.

Every ounce of energy that was expended to make you was transferred to you for your use. As the body possesses the potential to be sculpted by a committed body builder, so is your mind capable of being sculpted to its maximum potential if you commit to the workout necessary to do it.

Achieving your purpose is all on you. It is your choice. You have been given the ownership rights and afforded the discretion to do with your resources as you will.

It is your choice to use your mental chainsaw as a tool to chop down the forest that stands in your way, or you can use your mental chainsaw to tear up the things you were given stewardship over.

God forbid you use your gifts to take offense to everything your brother owns.

As owner you decide the use of the things you own. It is wise, in my estimation, to use those tools to affect your purpose. Any other use is vanity, and will be remembered by few and benefited by none.

Be great, My Nigga. It's what you were made to be.

Don't Worry. The Nigga Won't Read This.

"UP YE MIGHTY RACE. ACCOMPLISH WHAT YOU WILL."

" If you haven't confidence in self, you are twice defeated in the race of life."
Marcus Garvey

IT IS YOUR SEASON

Now is your time. I can not express enough, how important it is for you to make the choice and MOVE towards your purpose. There is so much for you to do...NOW!

Congratulations on proving me wrong and making it to the end of this book. Now that you are here, let me be the first to tell you that you have only just begun.

The interesting thing is, I will be on this journey with you. It wasn't many months ago that I was homeless, so you can rest easy knowing that what I am telling you is not theory, but practice.

This is my testimony.

Will you get a million dollars deposited into your account overnight? Probably not.

Will you awaken the giant in you overnight? Absolutely.

It took me selling out to my purpose, to find the strength necessary to write this book. It was write or die. I had to totally give in, to give up to my purpose.

You see, I believe that you and I were supposed to have this conversation. I believe that if I had not endured the losses that I have incurred, specifically, over the past few years, I would not be qualified to tell you that there is a giant on the inside of you that is waiting to take your world by storm.

Losing my business was necessary to qualify my purpose.

Getting a divorce was necessary to qualify my purpose.

Feeling the pain of lack and being driven into the wilderness of life was necessary to qualify my purpose.

So as you become aware of the sleeping giant in you, I want you to know that we have only just begun.

The secret to life is no secret at all. You are the secret.

In you lies the power to change and transform your situation in an instance.

You can turn the worst day of your life into the best day of your life because you know now that greater is He that is in you, than He that is in the world.

You know that you can call upon your giant to change every situation around you… NOW!

Your situation is just that… a situation. The odds are if it didn't kill you it will make you stronger. You're not dead…so get stronger.

Decide to change NOW and master yourself.

Strategically order your emotions. Now is the time to cause your emotions to work in your favor.

Every time the enemy comes in like a flood in your life, Call on the power that dwells in you to rise up, like a standard, and repel the enemy with an equal and opposite force.

When you call on your source, how could you stay depressed? When you decide to be happy and to let your power deal with the problems in your life how can you be anxious?

You are free to do just what you know you were called to do… LOVE.

In everything you do, do it as unto love.

Own who you are. Own where you are. Own where you are going.

Knowledge is key. Applied knowledge is POWER.

Learn how to master the POWER that lies inside of you to accomplish your defined purpose in life.

May Jah bless you tremendously,
Vic

Don't Worry. The Nigga Won't Read This.

FIND ME AT
WWW.FACEBOOK.COM/VGMAURICE

Special SHOUT OUT to my brother, MY NIGGA, my best friend, Danniell Battle.

I've met some awesome people along the way but I have yet to experience the type of Agape love from another person, that could mimic the way you so graciously pour into my life. You awe me every day dude, and I wanted you to know personally, that I AM MY BROTHERS KEEPER...Thanks for keeping me focused.

Let's do the same thing we do every day Danny...

TAKE OVER THE WORLD!

Love Ya...and be easy on the BUCK JUMPING!!! Lol

Made in the USA
Columbia, SC
12 May 2025